LANGUAGES
of the
SPIRIT

Developing Your Dictionary

MARLA MONK

Xulon
PRESS

Handwritten inscription:

KOURTNEY
...MISS KOURTNEY...
YOU ARE A WORLD CHANGER,
ATMOSPHERE SHIFTER, LEADER OF
LEADERS! THERE IS NO STOPPING YOU
& JESUS! YOUR WORSHIP REALLY
RELEASES HIS PRESENCE!
I LOVE YOU!
P. MARLA

Copyright © 2017 by Marla Monk

Languages of the Spirit
Developing Your Dictionary
by Marla Monk

Printed in the United States of America.

ISBN 9781498495752

Unless otherwise indicated, Scripture quotations taken from the Holman Christian Standard Bible (HCSB). Copyright © 1999, 2000, 2002, 2003, 2009 by Holman Bible Publishers, Nashville Tennessee. All rights reserved.

www.xulonpress.com

Dedication

This book is dedicated to my amazing husband, Dylan. You've always believed in me.

Acknowledgments

Dad and Mom – Thank you for your continual prayers and unwavering support. Dad, I can't thank you enough for a lifetime of imparted wisdom and rich insight.
Jakob – I love you, son! Your support has made my heart so happy!
Family and Friends – Thank you for your prayers and encouragement in this first-book journey!

Contents

Introduction

A picture speaks a thousand words.[1] The melody or harmony of a song can change your mood or heal your heart. A certain delicious scent can transport you to a past experience that you've long forgotten.

God speaks in many ways just like this. He uses all kinds of avenues to communicate with us. Sometimes, we have a hard time believing that He talks to us much at all, let alone the reality that He is *always* speaking. It's like a transistor radio. Hearing from Him simply requires that we find the right frequency. We can tune the dial of our hearts past the static and noise, until we find His station.

Learning to hear from God requires some fundamental truths: He loves you, He's always talking to You, He actually wants you to discover what He's saying, and He's inviting you into a partnership where He wants you to talk to others on His behalf, sharing His heart of love.

A common belief or misconception is that it's hard to understand what He's saying. It's true that He does speak mysteries. But He promises us in Jeremiah 33:3 that if we call to Him, make ourselves available to Him, He will tell us all about those mysteries! That's a promise. Just like learning to ride a bike or speak a new language, the more we practice the easier it becomes. As we cultivate our intimacy with God, we will begin to know more and more instinctively how He speaks to us individually and quickly be able to translate what He's communicating.

God loves to speak your language! Often, He uses metaphor, symbolism, or concepts that are very personalized to you. If you're a mechanic, He will use terms that you would only understand being in that line of work. If you're a computer programmer, He will often speak in technical language to convey a spiritual truth. If you're a stay-at-home mom, He will communicate in ways that are very practical or humorous to demonstrate His nurturing heart.

God doesn't want to frustrate us. He wants to be found by us. While we will never get to the end of discovering the depths of Him, He longs to make Himself known. Think about it like parenthood. Before a baby is even born, the parents talk to the big bump that will soon be their baby boy. They sing to him, pray for him, love and cherish the little life they haven't even yet seen, in the hopes he will be very familiar with their voices upon his arrival!

This is how God is towards us. Even when we were still sinners, He was thinking of us, talking to us, praying for us, loving and cherishing us, although we barely recognized or knew it was Him. How much more can we know, communicate with, and understand Him now that His Spirit lives inside us? He desperately wants us to find Him and understand what His heart feels towards us at a very intimate level.

Often what starts as an unfamiliar, counter-intuitive journey into hearing His voice, becomes a rhythm, a knowing, an intoxicating fragrance, and a technicolor landscape into which He invites us day-by-day.

This journey of learning the languages of the Spirit is also one of unlearning. Often our religious paradigms present constraints to going deeper in Him. Starting to become aware of these thoughts will help us relinquish limiting beliefs. Allowing the Holy Spirit to help us reshape our understanding of how He speaks will open up an amazing new world to enjoy and explore.

I remember for years I would struggle to connect with God because I had a religious misconception that meeting with Him required kneeling by my bed and praying for hours. It took many years, numerous great teachings, and lots of paradigm shifting to realize that He's with me wherever I go. I came to understand that communing with Him isn't relegated to a two-hour block of time in the morning. I'm not even a morning person, anyway! I usually connect best with Him at two in the afternoon. I soon realized that when it says in 1 Thessalonians 5:17 to "pray constantly" it would be completely ineffective for me to stay in my room kneeling by my bed all day if I'm to change the world. My prayer closet travels with me. I am a mobile sanctuary! Does this negate Matthew 6:6? Absolutely not. There is definitely a time and place to get alone with God. Jesus did it throughout His ministry and He is our example. What Jesus was addressing in that passage was religious show, empty facades, and prideful rituals. Our communication with God is to be authentic and personal.

Religion is diametrically opposed to the things of the Spirit. Religion vies for control. The Spirit gives freedom. Religion demands conformity. The Spirit celebrates individuality and uniqueness. Religion stifles. The Spirit permissions and creates. Religion brokers fear. The Spirit transforms in love. The list goes on and on. Often, when we bump up against a wall when desiring to go new places in God, a religious paradigm is suspect. We must let go of logic and religious rule-keeping. Once we do, we find that we are open to embracing the things of God even (and especially) if they don't make sense. 1 Corinthians 2:14 tells us the things of the Spirit can't be understood by the natural man anyway. It's impossible. Because the things of the Spirit are evaluated spiritually. Yet the irony in this process, as you'll see throughout this manual, is that the things of the Spirit are often discerned through our natural senses and developed through our creative imaginations. Ah, I love God. He enjoys messing with our inclination towards methods and the familiar.

Another key component of learning to understand the way God speaks at a greater level is knowing how loved you are by Him. It can sound so trite at times, a tired cliché or familiar bumper sticker. But it's true nonetheless. God loves you and will only speak to you through a heart of love. This is a good way to discern what you're hearing. Additionally, if we can move past how commonplace the word "love" is, how abused and misrepresented it is by our culture, and the reality that we may have become desensitized to the word "love," we can then start to grow in our understanding and experience of His *pure* love for us. It's hard to hear from a God we think is perverse, hates us, or is disappointed in us.

The Greek language had many different words for love, depending on the context in which it was used. If the context was sexuality, the Greeks used the word *eros*.[2] If brotherly love, the Greeks called it *philadelphos*.[3] When Jesus came on the scene, He introduced a new kind of love, *agapao*.[4] Jesus agapes you. He welcomes you. He is very, very pleased with you. He is at peace with you and chose a gruesome death to restore *you* back to His family. This is how loved you are.

Love is something to be experienced. The Bible tells us to "taste and see that the Lord is good."[5] It's hard to know that the Lord is good without *encountering* His goodness. I won't know how good a strawberry milkshake is just by looking at it. This is where theory has to be turned into experience. You can hand a Bible to an unsaved, deeply wounded person and say, "Everything you need to get freedom and healing is in here." While this statement is true, it's doubtful it will lead to any *real* change. Love must be experienced. The healing begins when we start to *apply* what the Bible says about God's great love to our lives. Experiencing His love for us is a journey of relationship in which we cultivate our story with Him, recording and remembering His faithfulness in our lives. This is why God told the Israelites to "remember" all that He'd done for them. If we aren't intentional about recognizing His faithful love in our lives, we will never apply the truth of the Bible to our experience and may relegate blessings to chance or the works of our own hands. He's good because the Bible says He is, but He's also good because I *know* He is.

God is not disappointed in you. He lives with a smile in His heart towards you. He belts out song at the top of His lungs and spins and dances all around heaven because of His great love for you (see Zephaniah 3:17). Encountering this great love is a process of renewing the mind from the lies that have been picked up throughout life. If you are riddled with fear, you can know that you have more renewing to do because the Bible says there is no fear in love. In fact, His perfect love casts out all fear.[6] When I have fear in my heart, I know His love must be perfected in me at a new level. In that same verse referenced above in Zephaniah, some translations say He will quiet us with His love. When our hearts and minds are so clamorous and chaotic, there is a place in His love that will quiet the voices of the enemy and calm the storm.

Knowing who we are in Christ is another big key for us to grow in hearing His voice. Often, the word used for this is "identity." When we fully begin to realize that at salvation Jesus moved in, that our old life was buried with Him in baptism, that we are afforded all the freedoms He purchased for us on the cross (love, peace, grace, healing, destiny, etc.), and that He's living in us to give us the fullest, most abundant life we could ever imagine, we start to become comfortable in our own skin. Jesus took care of every negative thing in our lives when He died on the cross. Everything. When He said "It is finished," He meant it. By His finished work and our application of that truth, our lives aren't ruled by the compulsions that used to drive us (shame, fear, anxiety, worry, anger, confusion, etc.). We can then start to embrace peace and rest as a lifestyle and hear from Him more clearly.

You are a son. You are a daughter. You are a child of the kindest Dad and friend of the greatest King to ever walk this planet. You share in His glorious inheritance and have a new address in heaven. Jesus has made you a royal priesthood, living in the earth to change the landscape to that of heaven. He trusts you! He loves your ideas! He wants to change this world with you!

As you'll discover walking through this manual, God is longing to communicate with us so we can set about the business of infiltrating and influencing every realm of society. As sons and daughters, kings and priests, we will take the Kingdom into all the world and shout with one voice, "The kingdoms of this world have become the kingdom of our God!"[7]

The world is dying for us to live in the fullness of this great Kingdom "on earth as it is in heaven"[8] life!

Living from Love

"By this all people will know that you are My disciples, if you have love for one another."
John 13:35

The more we learn about the gifts God has given us, the greater we can understand His world. God doesn't give us gifts to confuse us. He wants us to understand them and then go out and change the world with them! This is how we bring heaven to earth. It's how we make our world look like His.

Before we dive in, we're going to cover something very important that often gets overlooked or, dare I say, run over in our pursuit of spiritual gifts: love.

In 1 Corinthians 12 and 14, we have two amazing chapters that introduce and define spiritual gifts, their characteristics, and functions. But smack dab in the middle of the two chapters, is an entire chapter dedicated to love. Have you ever considered why? I like to call it the love sandwich. A sandwich isn't much of a meal without the meat. In fact, it would be very dull and dry at best, pointless at worst. That's how God sees spiritual gifts that He gives us. They are a key part of our Christian walk, but they are absolutely pointless if they're not used with a heart of love.

If I speak human or angelic languages
but do not have love,
I am a sounding gong or a clanging cymbal.

If I have the gift of prophecy
and understand all mysteries
and all knowledge,
and if I have all faith
so that I can move mountains
but do not have love, I am nothing.

And if I donate all my goods to feed the poor,
and if I give my body in order to boast
but do not have love, I gain nothing.

1 Corinthians 13:1-3

"Pursue love and desire spiritual gifts, and above all that you may prophesy."

1 Corinthians 14:1

In these verses, God reveals His heart regarding spiritual gifts. Before we desire the gifts of the Spirit, we are to run after love, chase it down, and apprehend it until it becomes a natural, constant expression in our lives. When gifts are expressed from a heart of love, it makes the fruit all the sweeter. In fact, we can't rightly use spiritual gifts or properly represent Jesus without love, because God is love.

God doesn't choose love. To say that He chooses to love implies that He can choose not to love, which is impossible. God *is* love. Love isn't a choice for Him, it's who He is. As we set out to discover and express the gifts He's given us, we have to understand that He wants us to use these gifts from a heart of love because they're meant to be an expression of Him.

Have you ever wondered why God heals people? I used to. This was a confusing topic for me at one time. Then, God spoke to my heart and told me it's one of the ways He demonstrates His love. Can you imagine having a life-long disease and then getting miraculously healed? This is a great understatement, but it would be like a kiss from Papa that He cares so deeply. His healing is an expression of His love.

It's good to take inventory of our motivators when pursuing the gifts. We may really want a gift of healing but it might be that we just want to wield influence. Or we may have a deep need for significance and think that if God would move through us in prophecy, we'd feel a sense of value or worth. But gifts have nothing to do with our identity. Our identity is in Christ. Gifts are meant to be an extension of God's love to His children.

The reality of it is, God doesn't need us to use spiritual gifts. He created the universe and holds it together by His word.[9] Yet, He chooses to partner with us to extend His Kingdom and spread His love throughout the world because He likes to spend time with us and delights in us experiencing His Kingdom here on earth. Jesus said that the world will know we belong to the One who *is* love when we, too, love. This is the genuine mark of a disciple of Jesus.

As quoted earlier, 1 Corinthians 13:2 says that I can prophesy 'til the cows come home and know all the mysteries of the galaxies, but if I don't have love, I *am* nothing. Note here that it doesn't say I *have* nothing or *do* nothing, it says I *am* nothing. The verb "to be" is about identity and state of existence. Simply put, what we do amounts to nothing in God's eyes when we do not love.

Following this bold statement, 1 Corinthians 14:1 reemphasizes the importance of love by telling us to pursue it. Love doesn't happen automatically. Often, love is the fruit of process, being refined and transformed into image of the One who *is* love. The word *pursue* is used in the Greek to figuratively mean a person who competes in a race to reach a goal, like a finish line.[10] Think about what it means to take on a good challenge. With my personality, if I'm going to compete in something, I want to make sure I can win. Otherwise, what's the point? This is what the Bible tells us to do: compete with one another in love. Can you imagine what it will be like when we as a Body fully realize that? While there is no competition in the Kingdom, the one thing God wants us to do is out-love each other!

I remember when my family first moved to Phoenix a handful of years ago, we stepped into all kinds of chaos. We knew the enemy was stirred up because we, as a family, were experiencing convergence. There's nothing the enemy hates more than people walking into the fullness of who they are and the purpose God has for them, let alone an entire family. Our car kept breaking down, our rental was filthy, missing a window, and the AC didn't work (it was July in Phoenix!). Meanwhile, my dad was having seizures back in California from fluid on his brain, some of my paintings were damaged in our move, we had to move into a hotel for two months (cockroaches included), all the while paying for the disgusting rental. We had to move our furniture and belongings into storage units, until the issues with the rental were settled, costing us even more money. We were bleeding thousands and thousands of dollars.

During this difficult transition, we had to file a change of address form from California, to the rental address in Phoenix, and then to a post office box until the rental issues got resolved. One day, I went to the post office box to pick up a package of movies my husband had ordered prior to our move. I opened our post office box to discover they were missing, although the website had indicated they had been successfully delivered. I marched into the post office and got (what I thought was) a very inept postal worker. He looked for the package for a long time and with every passing moment I got angrier. Finally, when he came back, I snapped. Just short of yelling, I asked him in a demeaning tone how hard it was to find a package!? I informed him that I'd worked in customer service for years and felt he had zero concept of what "customer service" really was. In a very snotty way, I accepted that the package was lost and stormed out.

Over the unfolding days, the Lord began to work in my heart. His sweet conviction set in and I realized that I was a terrible representative of Him that day. I felt horrible. I was in a leadership position in our ministry school, teaching our students on the importance of love, and failed miserably at the post office. God began to invite me into a process of transformation so that my character would look more like that of Jesus. He explained, through times of intimacy and revelation, how imperative it was to love like He does.

Later that year, I was walking up to one of our classrooms and I prayed under my breath, "God, I want to demonstrate Your power." Without skipping a beat, He said, "Demonstrate My love." I was stunned. He continued, "Love is the conduit through which My power flows." It took months and years to realize what He meant. He never wanted me to pursue the supernatural as a first priority. God revealed His heart to me about His desired order. Love first, spiritual gifts second. I came to realize that truly walking out a life of love is, indeed, super-natural. To love the person who just stabbed me in the back, for instance, requires a new nature. This love is the ultimate expression of the Kingdom. And it's from this place of love that God's power flows in miraculous ways to transform this hurting world. During this season, I discovered through the crucible of change, that the most authentic expression of my life as a follower of Jesus is love.

Reflection

This manual will cover many different types of spiritual giftings and experiences. It is designed to bring definition, context, and a greater understanding to the gifts that we each carry. This handbook is accompanied by reflections and activations at the end of each chapter to help turn theory into experience and give ample opportunity to practice! A key to learning is application.

1. Why is love so important in using spiritual gifts? _____

_____

2. In your own words, what does it mean to "pursue love?" _____

_____

_____

3. What revelations has God given you about His love? _____

_____

_____

Activation

Activation #1

Ask the Holy Spirit to show you or speak to your heart about someone that He wants you to express love and appreciation for. It can look like apologizing to someone or asking forgiveness for a bad attitude. Call someone on the phone you've been avoiding or write a kind word of thankfulness to someone for who they are and what they carry. Ask the Holy Spirit to help you. Whatever you do, be brave and be sincere.

Activation #2

Get alone with God and ask Him to show you three ways in which He demonstrates His love towards you. Write them down. Meditate on them. Let them sink into your heart. The more we know we're loved, the greater we can love.

Laying the Foundation

"Now about the gifts of the Spirit...I do not want you to be uninformed." (NIV)
1 Corinthians 12:1

Now that we've discovered the importance of love as our identity, we are going to lay a lot of groundwork, a foundation from which the rest of this manual will be built. There are treasures to mine as you walk through this workbook, but much of what you do with them is up to you. Teachers are called to equip the Body of Christ but each member is responsible for how much they learn and steward what they discover. The greater the stewarding, the greater the increase. Additionally, much of what is in this manual is a simplification of many topics. Each chapter could be an in-depth, stand-alone book. The goal of this manual is to make the languages of the Spirit evident and accessible to everyone through an introduction to the many ways God speaks.

My heart is that intentionality coupled with activation will result in your increased learning. In fact, I'm going to have you as the reader do an activation right at the beginning of this chapter. Go to the back of this manual to the "Holy Spirit Highlights/Notes" page. As you walk through this manual, write down the things that jump off the page or stand out to you. I often tell our students, "Pay attention to the things that get your attention." If the Holy Spirit emphasizes a word, a Scripture, or you "strangely" recall a childhood memory or song, write it down! You'll discover that this Holy Spirit prompting is often how God speaks to us (utilizing our gift of discernment). Additionally, the way He speaks is often customized to each person.

If there are things presented in this manual, words or concepts for instance that you don't understand, please seek them out further. Part of making our Christian walk authentic is to work out our *own* salvation. We can't rely on someone else to do it for us. Any area of our lives as a believer that is shrouded in mystery, insecurity, or even confusion is an invitation from the Lord to discover a deeper revelation.

When I was a newer Christian, I would sit and listen to great teachers and speakers but feel very insignificant, ignorant, or uneducated because I didn't understand the topics or words being discussed. As a result, my heart in this manual is also to build bridges and not obstacles. It's very important that we get answers to our questions because this is how we grow in maturity and understanding.

Whatever you do, don't disqualify yourself. Jesus is longing for you to embark on this journey of greater Kingdom discovery. Don't be afraid to pursue what you don't yet know. I would suggest to you that fear can be an indicator that you're right on track (with the caveat that fear is not always an indication of progress). When you're in a setting in which you can ask questions, I would encourage you to do so. I promise you, at least five other people have the same one but they're too afraid to ask. Be a pioneer! Lastly, cultivate community. Discussing the things of the Spirit with other Kingdom-minded believers will help you grow and learn in a safe place. We were never meant to be lone rangers.

Keys to Learning and Growing in Spiritual Gifts

Let's review some keys that will lay a foundation for this manual and help you grow in your spiritual gifts. While this is not an exhaustive list, these are keys that I have found helpful as I pursue my journey of becoming more intentional in my relationship with God and the discovery of His amazing world!

1. Position your heart to receive.

Expectation determines growth. To experience God and the spiritual realm on increasing levels we must position our hearts in a way that creates an expectation that we will receive. Think of it like creating a nest for the Holy Spirit in your heart. This nest is inviting to Him. It's in this place that He will show you new things and greater revelation. Additionally, much of positioning our hearts is about exercising faith that He's actually got gifts to give us. Hebrews 11:6 says, "And without faith it is impossible to please God, because anyone who comes to Him must believe that He exists and that He rewards those who earnestly seek Him." Position your heart to seek Him and you will receive.

2. Approach the Kingdom like a little child.

Mark 10:15 says, "I assure you: Whoever does not welcome the kingdom of God like a little child will never enter it." The things of the Kingdom are best received with childlikeness. What are some childlike qualities you can think of?

Faith, trust, fun, and curiosity are characteristics of little kids. Many times, children can implicitly trust and accept the things of God because they don't have baggage or skepticism. Their immediate heart's answer is "yes"! Does this mean we are to blindly accept every wind of doctrine and teaching out there? No. But this is where we've got to ask and trust the Holy Spirit! He will guide us into all truth.[11] While there is definitely a time to be a Berean, our heart position is to be one of faith, not unbelief.

Additionally, I don't want you to agree with everything I share in this manual. I would encourage you to seek out the things that don't sit right, cause alarms to go off inside of you, or raise more questions than answers. This demonstrates that you're processing and learning. Search the Scriptures and talk with the Lord. He'll bring clarity and, perhaps, revelation I haven't yet received!

3. Don't be afraid to ask questions.

Did you know that God is not afraid of your questions? It's religion that would make you feel like you can't question the things of God. Religion wants you to shut up and obey. However, the more you ask, the more you'll learn! Be an investigator into the things of God. He has so much that He wants to show you. He's got answers to questions you haven't even yet asked! Whatever you don't understand in your learning journey, put on a shelf. Don't let it be an obstacle. If you have an objection pop into your head while you're learning, write it down. Don't struggle with it to the point of losing momentum or squelching revelation. Ask questions about it, for sure, but don't let it hinder learning. Questions demonstrate curiosity.

4. Be intentional about turning theory into experience.

As I mentioned earlier, God wants to take our theory and turn it into experience. A popular quote says it beautifully, "A man with an experience is never at the mercy of a man with an argument."[12] I remember I was working in sales many years ago, and another sales rep wanted to argue the Bible with me. At that point in time, I wasn't very skilled in the Word and told him very softly, "I don't know a lot of the verses you're referencing, but what I can tell you about is what God has done in my life." I proceeded to share my testimony with him and he completely relaxed and began to listen. That day, we could have argued theology but authenticity came through my experience with Jesus.

Our encounters with God will provide a genuine trust in Him, our Anchor, when the storms of life come. As soon as things get tumultuous, we can lean into Him, remembering our experiences with His faithfulness. Then, we can weather anything life throws at us. We can draw from our history with Him, knowing that He's always come through. Head knowledge robs us of authenticity. When theory graduates to experience, the Holy Spirit can move in greater power in and through our lives.

5. Carry a heart of humility.

Humility captures God's heart. Numbers 12:6-7 tells us that while God speaks to prophets in visions and dreams, Moses actually got to see the form of the Lord because of his faithfulness to God. In verse 3 of that same chapter, a component of Moses' faithfulness is revealed. The Bible says that "Moses was a very humble man, more so than any man on the face of the earth." From his example, we can see that posturing our hearts with humility will lead to increased encounters.

6. The Holy Spirit will not contradict the Word.

One commonfear I come across with students is a worry that in the exploration process they will be deceived or lead astray by something that is not of God. Remember, the enemy often uses a tactic of fear to get us off the scent by which the Holy Spirit is leading us. The best way to know if God is inviting you into a learning journey is to talk to Him. He is a kind and gentle Shepherd and will not lead you astray. It's important to remember that while God will never contradict His word, He will often seek to dismantle religious paradigms that present obstacles to new revelation. This paradigm-shifting can be scary because we may have old beliefs we've lived with for a long time! Also, being in a community of Kingdom-minded believers will offer safety (see Proverbs 11:14), dialogue, and accountability.

7. Believe that God wants you to grow in Spiritual things!

Can you imagine a dad who wraps a bunch of Christmas gifts for his children, puts them under the tree, but doesn't ever let his kids open them? That would be crazy! God gives us gifts because He wants us to open them, explore them, grow in them, and use them. Every good gift comes from God (see James 1:17). His heart is that we would become familiar with His nature and the things of His Kingdom to partner with Him in extending His government around the globe. Even if you don't feel like anything is happening as you're learning, believe that you're receiving and that the Holy Spirit will bring increased understanding. It's good to remember that our Christian walk is one of faith. Faith is not an emotion, so feelings aren't an accurate measurement of growth. Much of Kingdom growth springs from belief.

8. Stewarding is a key to increase.

What God has for you in your future, He is equipping you with now. In looking back through my own journals, I see a consistent preparing in a previous season for what I stepped into in the next. God gave me tools, keys, principles, and even prophetic answers to questions I wouldn't yet ask for two years!

Be intentional about collecting, recording, and nurturing what He gives you so that you can be greater equipped as you move forward in your call. Steward the insights and revelation He shares by journaling them, meditating on them, and asking Him about them. Remember the parable of the talents? The two managers who invested the money given to them, doubled their investments, and were given charge over *cities* for their good stewardship! How's that for increase?

9. You are qualified!

Jesus is the One who gives gifts, not man. Don't ever let anyone make you feel as if you are disqualified. And don't let lies of insecurity find a home in your thought life. Jesus is the One who qualifies you and He will never apologize for doing so (see Romans 11:29)! Often we think, "Oh, I can't prophesy like so-and-so," or "I don't have a gift like him or her." When we do this, we can actually stop up the gifts! Trying to determine who's qualified and who's not is a form of comparison, which is ultimately rooted in pride. Additionally, the Bible wouldn't tell us to desire spiritual gifts if they weren't available to all of us. Imagine the spiritual gifts, experiences, and journeys we miss out on because we don't pursue them due to perceived or assumed disqualification.

10. Be open to getting rid of old paradigms/ways of thinking.

As mentioned in the introduction of this manual, old paradigms can be hazardous to growth. Self-awareness and openness to change can be beneficial in reshaping our belief systems. With an open heart, we can embrace new wineskins (ways of thinking) and receive new wine (revelation). A good litmus test for discovering old paradigms within us is how vehemently we protect our doctrine and beliefs.

11. Ask God to help you look through new lenses.

Often distorted lenses come from past wounds, hurts, and experiences. Many people have shied away from spiritual gifts because they've been hurt by abuse of the prophetic, for instance. The enemy leverages these negative experiences when we set out to explore and use spiritual gifts. He aims to keep us from the inherent fruit and freedom God intended as a by-product of their proper use. Many an inner vow has been made by believers who were hurt by their last church: "I will never do that again!" or "I will never let anyone prophesy over me again!" This is exactly what the enemy wants. However, God can redeem and restore any bad experiences you've had. Invite Him to heal you from any hurt or wound caused by misuse, control, or manipulation. Ask Him to show you the great value of the gifts He's given you. His fresh, new lens will help you see the purpose and joy of operating in them.

12. We absolutely don't do fear.

There is to be no fear in the discovery process. What I mean by that is, don't allow fear to wreak havoc as you learn. The two don't mix. The learning journey is meant to be an adventure! If you begin to feel fear at any point in the process, it can mean a number of things: faulty assumptions are being made, truth is bumping up against old paradigms, or the enemy is trying to scare you away from an immense breakthrough. The Bible tells us there is no fear in love.[13] If you begin to feel fear rise up at any point just ask God about it. Don't let the fear distract you from receiving revelation or having fun in the exploration process! Inviting God in by asking questions will allow Him to greater demonstrate His love towards you and it will allow you to experience His joy as you discover the gifts He's given you.

The Journey of Developing Your Dictionary

This whole journey of learning to hear how God speaks is one that is very intimate and customized. Often, we can think that we must prophesy or exercise a gift of healing like the last anointed teacher we just heard. But the truth is, God has a very tailored way of speaking to and flowing through each one of us. We discover that the more authentic we are with the gifts He's given us, the more His anointing can uniquely move through us.

Below, we will discover some tools and resources to help us grow in hearing God's voice. But, remember, He often has a way of speaking that is quite unique to each individual. The more we equip ourselves with knowledge and God gives us insight and revelation, the greater we can develop our own personal dictionaries. As we do we, in turn, find that we don't need to heavily rely on commentaries, resources, or seek out other people to prophesy over us, because we have a growing confidence in knowing that we can hear from Him ourselves.

Let's face it, it's easy to lean on other's interpretations of Scripture, symbolism, or metaphor. But God longs to spend time with us and disclose revelation that is highly personalized and potentially new! As you set out to discover what He's saying to you, ask the Holy Spirit for His guidance and fresh revelation.

The Rule of First Mention

When trying to understand what a certain symbol, word, or number means, we can often use the rule of first mention. The rule of first mention is a guideline that many people use to better understand the nature or characteristics of something from the Bible. It simply means that the first time a number, color, object, etc. is mentioned in the Word, we can get understanding for what it represents or means by the context and usage in which it was first introduced.

For instance, if I have a vision of a serpent, I can use this rule to help me discover what God is saying by searching it out in the Word. The first time "serpent" is used in the Bible is in Genesis 3:1, "Now the serpent was the most cunning of all the wild animals that the Lord God had made." So, I discover in this verse that the nature of the serpent is to be crafty, stealthy, and scheming in his process of deceiving. Then, I can apply the knowledge that I've just learned to the vision I've received and ask God what He'd like me to do with what I've discovered (usually a vision like this will involve intercession to birth the solution, thwart a scheme of the enemy, or break bondage).

If we solely rely on the rule of first mention, however, we see that it becomes problematic once God starts speaking to us through modern-day images and pictures like cell phones and computers. This rule is a great guideline, but ceases to be helpful with contemporary imagery. With pictures that aren't in the Word, ask Holy Spirit and friends for their insight.

Books and Resources

There are fantastic Christian books, resources, and teachings out there on many spiritual things. Dream interpretation, for instance, is a widely-published topic. Even in the field of psychology, we can see commonalities that overlap with spiritual definitions in dream imagery. Utilizing a vast array of resources can aid us in our journey of translating what the Spirit is saying and help us build our own dictionaries.

Training Your Spirit

Part of this journey in hearing from God is about training our spirits to become aware of and comfortable with the things of the Spirit. The Bible says the flesh profits nothing, but the Spirit gives life.[14] So, anything we learn, receive, and cultivate in the Spirit will have eternal fruit and abundant life. Often training our spirits is really about acclimating the rest of our person (body and soul) to what our spirits already know. The more we are intentional about cultivating the Spirit life, the more we begin to realize that we were most likely intuitively already operating in this realm to some degree.

John 4:24 says, "God is spirit, and those who worship Him must worship in spirit and truth." I'd like to suggest that we not only worship Him in Spirit but we can explore Him and enjoy Him in Spirit, as well. This Spirit-life is meant to be our new identity, the foundation from which our life in Christ is built. When we get saved, the Bible tells us that a critical process of transformation must happen. This process is renewing the mind (see Romans 12:2). The old mind cannot accept and comprehend the things of God (see 1 Corinthians 2:14). So, we must renew our minds to align with the Word and what our spirits instinctively embrace. Our mind says, "Whoa, wait a minute! This is weird." Our spirit says, "Trust." Our mind permissions distractions, our spirit seeks communion with God and delights in being led by Him. Our mind wants to dominate, our spirit loves to yield.

This transition from soul to spirit is one of maturity. Hebrews 5:14 says, "But solid food is for the mature—for those whose senses have been trained to distinguish between good and evil." There's a lot we can break down in this verse but it's important to note that the Bible makes a distinction between immaturity and maturity in our Christian walk. God forever invites us into a process of maturation. The power of the human will, however, is that we can choose whether or not we want to continue in our transformation process. Maturity is available, but it's also a choice.

In this passage in Hebrews, the Greek word for *senses,* from the root word *aisthanomai*, translates "by the bodily senses."[15] It's interesting to note that our senses are actually utilized in discerning the things of the Spirit. Additionally, the word *trained* in this verse is the word *gymnazo:* very similar to the word *gymnasium*. This word defined means "to exercise vigorously, in any way, either the body or the mind."[16]

Putting all this together, we can see that exploring things of the Spirit involves our bodily senses and our mind in perceiving. This can be a bit tricky if we're really wounded. The transformation process, then, becomes imperative. We are spirit, soul, and body (see 1 Thessalonians 5:23) and this is the proper order for our lives. When we're out of alignment with this God-given order, or have gaping soul wounds, or filthy minds, we can often view the things of the Spirit in a very distorted way. Our soul, which is the culmination of mind, will, and emotions[17] is meant to be secondary to our spirit because it often operates out of hurts, history, and agenda. Our renewed mind is beautiful, creative, and powerful, but it's still meant to be led by our spirit.[18]

You might be asking, "Well, how am I supposed to discern with my spirit, using my mind and bodily senses if I need healing?" The short answer: it's a process. But know that God's desire is for your whole person to be in sync, healthy, and whole, ever growing towards maturity. The greater healing that you receive and the more your mind is renewed, the greater freedom your spirit will have to be lead of the Holy Spirit.

Your Native Language with the Spirit

The languages of the Spirit have commonalities but they are also highly personal. Make a practice of talking with the Holy Spirit about what He's saying specifically to you regarding symbolism and metaphor as you study the Word, have dreams, and experience visions. Throw out absolutes and be open to new interpretations breathed by the Spirit directly to you. Psalm 42:7 says, "Deep calls unto deep." God is constantly drawing us, longing to talk to each one of us uniquely and specifically about our relationship with Him, our families, our jobs, and our lives in a Spirit-to-spirit manner.

God loves to speak your language! As mentioned earlier, He doesn't want to confuse you and will often communicate in ways that correspond with your vocation or hobbies to make this communication process easy and fun. The more intentional you are about stewarding what He gives you, the more He will show you, and the greater you will instinctively know what He's saying.

During one season of my life, the Lord kept showing me the number "444." If I had held to or relied on a common interpretation, I would have thought He was talking to me about the four corners of the earth or creation. In doing so, I would never have received a full revelation of what He was trying to intimately speak to my heart. But as I began to ask God what He was saying, He told me He was laying and establishing a new foundation in my life (think four corners of a floor). I had been dealing with some familiar fear and anxiety and this word from Him brought great comfort and hope that He was doing a fresh thing. Had I depended on the go-to interpretation instead of seeking Him out first, I wouldn't have received this personalized, timely word from Him.

In another season, I had a dream with a big sign, like a billboard, revealing certain numbers and words specific to the line of work I was in (I will go into more detail of this dream in the manual). When I woke up from the dream, I knew immediately what God was communicating because it was a native language to me. Had I sought out popular resources or relied on other people to interpret for me, I never would have gotten the tailored message from God, built my dictionary further, or understood at a deeper level that He loves to communicate with me in a way that is highly personalized.

Defining Spiritual Gifts

We've covered some keys to growing in spiritual gifts, different resources, principles, and tools. Now that we've laid a framework for growing in the things of the Spirit, let's define the Spiritual gifts as laid out in 1 Corinthians chapter 12.

"1 Now concerning spiritual gifts, brethren, I do not want you to be ignorant: 2 You know that you were Gentiles, carried away to these dumb idols, however you were led. 3 Therefore I make known to you that no one speaking by the Spirit of God calls Jesus accursed, and no one can say that Jesus is Lord except by the Holy Spirit. 4 There are diversities of gifts, but the same Spirit. 5 There are differences of ministries, but the same Lord. 6 And there are diversities of activities, but it is the same God who works all in all. 7 But the manifestation of the Spirit is given to each one for the profit of all: 8 for to one is given the word of wisdom through the Spirit, to another the word of knowledge through the same Spirit, 9 to another faith by the same Spirit, to another gifts of healings by the same Spirit, 10 to another the working of miracles, to another prophecy, to another discerning of spirits, to another different kinds of tongues, to another the interpretation of tongues. 11 But one and the same Spirit works all these things, distributing to each one individually as He wills." (NKJV)

1 Corinthians 12:1-11

In this passage, Paul introduces us to the gifts of the Spirit. At the outset of this passage, he communicates that he desires for the reader to not be "ignorant." As discussed earlier in this chapter, growing in the things of God requires intentionality and is a journey into maturity. We'll break these gifts down at a simple level in just a moment, but first I'd like to point out verse four:

"There are diversities of gifts, but the same Spirit."

The word "gift" here is from the root *charis* in the Greek, which translates: *grace*.[19] Depending on your Bible translation, you may also see the word "one" in relation to whom the Spirit gives gifts. I would encourage you to re-evaluate the word "one," look it up in your concordance, and ask the Holy Spirit to give you insight about this word. The problem is, in many religious environments, we as believers have been told that not everybody can have the same gift. This is usually supported by verses that follow this passage regarding many members of one Body, each with a separate function. However, this is a misinterpretation. The first passage relates to gifts, the second relates to religious or vocational function. When the gifts are rigidly, and erroneously, relegated to certain individuals, it begs the question: "Who gets to decide who the special 'one' in the church is to prophesy or heal?"

As you can see, not only is this passage misinterpreted but pride is suspect in this line of reasoning. The Holy Spirit is the One who decides how and when He'd like to distribute gifts. I would like to suggest that they are available to us all.

If we go back to the word *charis,* we can look at the spiritual gifts like we each have a grace. I have a grace on my life for carrying, using, and imparting certain essences of the gifts and so do you. Although we may operate in all the gifts, our graces and flavors will certainly be different.

I hope you're still tracking with me. What I'm not saying is that we determine the gifts we receive. That's the Holy Spirit's job. Also, I'm not saying that certain people don't have a greater grace than others. We can look to the generals of the past, for instance, and see that each of their lives were marked by certain anointings and mantles. What I am saying is that if Jesus is our example, and He operated in all the gifts, then all the gifts are available to us by legal access of the cross.

The Holy Spirit gives to every person affectionately, as and when He wills, and these gifts can manifest in any number of ways as the occasion calls for. Let me give you an example. I am wired more for the prophetic. Other people I know are wired more for supernatural healing and laying on of hands. When I step into a corporate setting, I'm usually operating from two places: extending the Kingdom and impregnating the environment with prophecy. Those wired for healing are scanning the room for wheelchairs and crutches. Does this mean they don't prophesy? No. Does this mean I can't lay my hands on the sick? No. Jesus said that I will lay hands on the sick and they will recover.[20] Jesus didn't qualify that verse by saying, "Only those with the gift of healing can lay hands on the sick."

When we walk into a room, we are to be in tune with what the Holy Spirit is doing. Remember, Jesus only did what He saw His Father doing. Can you imagine if Jesus saw that God's heart was to heal someone but His reply to His Dad was that He couldn't operate in healing because He didn't have the "gift?" We can apply this same principle to ourselves. When we are sensitive to what God is doing in a room, and we've created a new wineskin in our doctrine that any one of us can operate in any of the gifts, we make ourselves completely available to God to do anything He wants to do through us at any given time!

Breaking Down the Gifts

1. Word of Wisdom

A word of wisdom is a timely message from the Spirit of God for a person that is usually strategic and can help with directional guidance. It also aids in the interpretation of dreams.[21] I believe directional words are best given and received by people you are in community with and have accountability to. However, be open to the prompting and manifestation of the Spirit in communicating words of wisdom.

2. Word of Knowledge

A word of knowledge is information that you get about someone else or a situation that you couldn't have known naturally. For instance, if I meet someone in the line at Starbucks and I get an impression that they live on a street called "Rogers Lane" and that person confirms it, I have just received knowledge about them directly from God. There's no way in the natural I could have known that they live on that street. The Holy Spirit is the One who gave me that information.

Often when I operate in words of knowledge, they are wrapped up in a prophetic word. I usually find out after the delivery of the word that part of it included specific information about the person's life. I rarely have understanding beforehand that I'm getting a word of knowledge. I have come to know that God doesn't show me, personally, ahead of time that it's a word of knowledge because I am prone to pride in my life. I believe that if I often had foreknowledge, I'd try to make a business of it or be tempted to puff myself up through self-promotion.

Often the purpose, and fruit, of a word of knowledge is to open the hearts of people. When someone hears from a complete stranger a detail of their life that there is absolutely no way the speaker could have known, the hearer realizes, at some level, they've just had an encounter with a supernatural God who knows them and loves them.

3. Faith

This gift is defined as the "conviction of the truth of anything, belief; a conviction or belief respecting man's relationship to God and divine things, generally with the included idea of trust and holy fervor born of faith and joined with it."[22] In other words, this faith is demonstrated by you believing who God says He is and believing that He can provide anything needed in any situation because the Word says He can. This is a logic defying, hope-inspiring, in-the-face-of-all-odds faith. Heaven celebrates hearts positioned with implicit trust.

4. Healing

This word means healing, remedy, or medicine. It's from the Greek root word *iaomai,* which means to cure, heal, or make whole.[23] An example of this is in Matthew 8 when the centurion told Jesus that if He'd just send His word, his paralyzed servant would be healed. It's important to note that the centurion's faith paved a way for the healing of his servant.

5. Working of Miracles

This is the operational power and ability to perform miracles. An example of this is the woman with the issue of blood in Luke chapter 8. When the woman touched the edge of Jesus' garment, He actually felt the power drain out of Him. The Greek phrase for working of miracles is *energēma dynamis.*[24] She was healed by His miracle-working power. Another example of working of miracles is in Luke 4. Jesus was in the synagogue and cast out a demon. The people were amazed and wondered by what power He performed this. As we can see from these two passages, the power to work miracles often accompanies healing and deliverance.

6. Prophecy

Prophecy is defined as "a discourse emanating from divine inspiration and declaring the purposes of God...comforting the afflicted, or revealing things hidden; esp. by foretelling future events."[25] It has two components: one who speaks forth the things of God, such as revelation about the

Kingdom; and foretelling, which is simply prophesying future events. We will dive deeper into this gift in the prophecy chapter.

7. Discerning of Spirits

This word here for discern is *diakrisis* in the Greek and is defined as a "distinguishing or a judging of spirits."[26] 1 Corinthians 14:29 says, "Two or three prophets should speak, and the others should evaluate." Discerning of spirits and judging a prophetic word come from the same root meaning, *diakrinō*: "To separate, make a distinction, discriminate, to prefer, or to learn to discern or judge."[27] Discernment is a gift given by the Spirit to help us evaluate what's happening in the spirit realm and help us determine if what we're sensing is from God, another spirit, or human flesh. As you'll see in the next chapter, I believe that discernment is one of the most operational gifts in each of us as believers. The awareness, strength, and usage of the gift develops through maturation.

8. Different Kinds of Tongues (Languages)

The word tongues is *glossa*. It is defined as "a tongue or the language or dialect used by a particular people distinct from that of other nations," specifically, "one naturally unacquired."[28] In other words, one doesn't get Rosetta Stone software to learn these languages, the Holy Spirit downloads them directly.

9. Interpretation of Tongues

This means the ability, by the Holy Spirit, to interpret what is spoken by unknown tongues.[29]

Thoughts on the Gifts

An error that I believe we've made as a church is over-categorizing and compartmentalizing these gifts. I believe we've wrongly and staunchly, at times, said that they are all in separate boxes and used independently of one another. Categorizing, or putting rules around something of the Spirit, has its roots in legalism.

It's been my experience that many gifts of the Spirit are interrelated and interconnected. For instance, I can *discern* that the Holy Spirit wants me to give a prophecy to someone because that person is highlighted to me. Then as I go *prophesy* God's heart of love and plans for them, the Holy Spirit gives me *words of knowledge* that I could not have known in order to open up their heart like a flower. Finally, as I prophesy, my hands get hot and I know the Holy Spirit wants to *heal* them of an illness.

Again, I believe we as a church have also incorrectly taught or implied that only certain people get certain gifts. But it's the Spirit who distributes the spiritual gifts of God to every person deliberately, willingly, and affectionately. The Holy Spirit is strategic and purposeful. He has a plan, He gives gifts according to His plan, and He does so affectionately and joyously. He gives these gifts to us with love from His heart.

If we pull back the curtain, then, we find that often pride or elitism are culprits in rigidly defining and interpreting these gifts. Human agenda has inserted itself between the Word and the Spirit. For instance, you may have heard certain church leaders in your past say that "Only the prophet of the house can prophesy," or "Go to sister-so-and-so if you want healing." This is irresponsible and, dare I say, unbiblical. The Bible says we can all prophesy and Jesus told us that if we lay hands on the sick, they *will* recover. That's a promise. Now, it's true that we can't all be prophets. That's for certain because the office of prophet is a *call* from God and no one can self-appoint (see Ephesians 4:11-16). But as you will see in the following chapters, these gifts are available to everyone and the Giver of the gifts already lives inside of you!

Extending the Kingdom

I love to connect dots. At some point, you may ask what these languages of the Spirit and the spiritual gifts are even for. It's actually quite simple. We're to use the gifts God has given us to change the world. You see, wherever we go, the Kingdom goes and wherever the Kingdom goes, gifts manifest to make any environment look more like heaven.

I don't know what your eschatology is, but some of what you'll learn in this manual is to understand the purpose of spiritual things within the larger context of the world. Eschatology is just a fancy word for what one believes about the end of the world from a Biblical perspective.

Did you know that what we believe about the end times determines how we live today? If we believe that the world will end in a fiery dystopia, it's doubtful that we will have much hope for our today or any motivation to use the spiritual gifts God has given us to change the world. If it's all going to hell in a handbasket what difference can we really make anyway?

But if we have a Kingdom eschatology and don't believe the earth will end in destruction, if we aren't looking for a cloud to hop on to escape this horrible world, we can actually begin to believe that we are partners with God to extend His Kingdom throughout the earth! Much of the end is up to us. God is looking for Kingdom-minded believers who will work with Him to change the landscape of earth to that of heaven.

Jesus is coming back to a celebration not a dystopia! Isaiah 2: says, "In the last days the mountain of the Lord's house will be established at the top of the mountains and will be raised above the hills. All nations will stream to it..." As we go out into all the world and infiltrate every realm of influence, people will begin to see that we carry Kingdom answers. In the end, all nations will come in celebration to the Answer. We have the Hope inside of us this world is crying out for. It's Christ in us, the hope of glory!

Isaiah 60:1-3 says it like this, "Arise, shine, for your light has come, and the glory of the Lord shines over you. For look, darkness covers the earth, and total darkness the peoples; but the Lord will shine over you, and His glory will appear over you. Nations will come to your light, and kings to the brightness of your radiance."[30] Nations are dying for the hope and light of Christ in you because Jesus is the only sustainable, real answer for the world's problems.

In Isaiah 9:7 we see a promise. It says, "Of the increase of His government and peace there will be no end." (NKJV) You're here to extend God's government, His Kingdom, here in the earth! It's a guarantee. And His Kingdom is always extended through a heart of peace. When Jesus, the Prince of Peace, prayed "On earth as it is in heaven," it wasn't just an idea. It was *the* way to pray, *the* way to align with God's plans and purposes for this earth, *the* blueprint for change. As a side note, what I love about this verse is that it gives us insight into how Jesus prayed and how He positioned His heart while He was here on the earth!

Our job, then, is to bring heaven to earth in cooperation with God by using the spiritual gifts He's given us, through a heart of love and lifestyle of peace. Mark 16:20 says, "And they went out and preached everywhere, the Lord working *with* them and confirming the word by the accompanying signs." (emphasis added)

Regarding spiritual gifts, remember that it's the Holy Spirit who gives and it's the Holy Spirit who anoints, always with a strategic purpose. Gaining experience and growing in the supernatural isn't just for us to have deep metaphysical and mysterious encounters with God. While He does love for those experiences to happen in times of intimacy with us, spiritual gifts and operating in the languages of the Spirit is primarily about giving His lost children, our cities, and the nations of the world life-changing, course-altering encounters with God. It's not enough for us to keep the supernatural to ourselves. Stories will be rewritten through salvation, deliverance, healing, signs and wonders as we partner with God to use the gifts He's given us.

Lastly, we don't use and exercise the gifts of the Spirit through willpower. The Holy Spirit moves on our lives as we yield to Him continuously, dialogue with Him, and ask Him what He'd like to do through us, in season and out of season. Using the gifts is about availability. Isaiah 10:27 says, "And the yoke will be destroyed because of the anointing oil." (NKJV) Yokes of bondage are broken and lives are changed *by* the Holy Spirit *through* surrendered vessels like you and me! This is Kingdom partnership. It's allowing the Kingdom to flow through us in any situation, any environment, at any time. God's heart aches for all His kids to know the *real* Him, the One who is kind and loving, the One who heals all diseases and breaks all yokes. God is longing to empower you by His Spirit to demonstrate heavenly realities to the hurting world until every last area looks identical to His Kingdom.

Reflection

1. How does the Holy Spirit often move through you? _____

_____

2. What spiritual gifts do you long to operate in? _____

_____

3. Why does "qualification" have its roots in pride? _____

_____

4. How has your understanding of the purpose of spiritual gifts changed? _____

_____

Activation

Activation #1

Take one of the items you wrote down at the back of the manual that the Holy Spirit highlighted to you from this chapter. Ask Him to show or tell you more about it. Once He does, ask Him what He'd like you to do with what He's shown you.

Activation #2

Ask Jesus, "What's your favorite thing about me?" Write down the first things that come to mind or pictures you receive. Go with your gut.

Activation #3

Begin to develop your own dictionary using the following chart:

Sign/Symbol/Number/Impression/Color	Definition
My Example: 444	*God says He's bringing stability to my life. Four corners of a foundation. "4" three times means God, Jesus, and Holy Spirit are in agreement!*

Discernment

"A demonstration of the Spirit is given to each person to produce what is beneficial...[including] distinguishing between spirits.*"*
1 Corinthians 12:7, 10 (parenthesis added)

Discernment is one of the gifts of the Spirit that I believe is the most common and operational in the life of a believer. Discernment is something that can often be traced back to childhood. Without realizing it, we've used discernment to help us navigate many situations intuitively before we knew what the gift was or, perhaps, before we were even saved.

I remember when I was about seven years old, I saw a chubby little demon up in the corner of a room. At the time, I didn't know exactly what it was, but I knew it was bad. Interestingly, although I was plagued with fear most of my life, I don't recall this experience being fearful. Another time as a young child, I was around an adult that didn't "feel" safe to me. I couldn't explain it then, but I was discerning that this person had something negative working in their life.

I would suggest to you that every person has spiritual sensitivities because God knitted us in our mother's womb, and every person is born with a spirit. We all, at some level, instinctively know certain things, although we may not have language in which to describe what we're sensing or experiencing. Now, are these sensitivities or "gifts" redeemed before someone gets saved? No. But that doesn't mean they aren't there. It just means that, unfortunately, they can get skewed and, certainly, misunderstood while they are being used through the filter of the flesh. Sometimes these sensitivities can feel overwhelming because they aren't used with the guidance of the Holy Spirit and, in turn, can get shut down. Until we come into relationship with Jesus these gifts will always be a bit distorted. When we get saved, the Holy Spirit breathes His redemptive life on us and we connect with God's plans and purposes over our lives. This includes a proper alignment - spirit, soul, and body. When our gifts are used in partnership with the Holy Spirit, through a healthy, redeemed soul, the outcome has immense Kingdom power and eternal consequence.

In this chapter, we are going to define and unpack the discernment gift and learn how it works with other spiritual gifts. My heart is that you will become more aware of the gifts and graces that you carry and that this chapter will help you see how the gift of discernment works (and to some extent, has always worked) in your life.

The Basics of Discernment

As we saw in the previous chapter, 1 Corinthians 12:4 says that we each have gifts that the Lord distributes. He gives these gifts affectionately and with love in His heart. The definition in the Greek means a different distribution to different persons.[31]

Did you know that the Lord has given you specific graces He may not have given your pastor or best friend? Did you also know that if He's given you a gift of discernment and your best friend a gift of discernment it will most likely be perceived, experienced, and expressed in completely different ways? We were all created uniquely. We have different personalities and strengths. If I were to give 12 different people a blank canvas, the same color paints, and told them to all paint the same specific picture, each and every one would look different.

God celebrates diversity and uniqueness. He's not looking for robots. He doesn't want to program us so we just go out and regurgitate everything He tells us. He wants us to have authentic experiences with Him that we can share with the world, expressed through the personalities He's given us. When we realize we're permissioned to be who God created us to be, our lives will have an undeniable genuineness about them and the anointing of the Holy Spirit can flow more freely.

While there are certainly some commonalities in experiences, we each have a way of discerning that is unique, customized, and instinctive. Additionally, the gift of discernment has often been used to try and perceive every negative thing in an environment. However, this gift can operate in so many different amazing ways. An increased awareness and intentionality in growing in the gift can help us better understand how it works in our lives.

Keys to Growing in Discernment

There are some basic keys that have helped me grow more in discernment. As you read through this section, the Holy Spirit may prompt you with other ways to grow in your unique gift. Use the Holy Spirit highlights section at the end of this manual to record and explore them with the Lord.

1. Be available.

Partnering with the Holy Spirit in the gifts He's given us is about being available. It's not about being the best or greatest. God is just looking for people who will say "yes"! As we mature and grow in our walk with the Lord we begin to learn that our Christian life is not all about ourselves. Please note: I am not promoting a self-deprecating, lowly worm doctrine here. God created us as powerful people with a divine purpose. But as we grow and mature, we begin to realize that there is a world out there dying to know His goodness. He constantly invites us, as sons and daughters, into a place of availability so we can use our spiritual gifts to partner with Him to heal this hurting world and demonstrate His love!

2. Stay sharp.

Another key to understanding and utilizing spiritual gifts is what I call "staying sharp." This is the process of being clear mentally, emotionally, and physically and is very important in discerning spiritual things. Ecclesiastes 10:10 says, "If the ax is dull, and one does not sharpen its edge, then one must exert more strength; however, the advantage of wisdom is that it brings success." Wisdom is knowing that we won't have to work so hard if our ax is sharp! For instance, if I'm full of anxiety and walk into an environment where there is a spirit of fear, I won't know if what I'm discerning is my own issue or if it's predominantly in the atmosphere.

Wisdom for me, in this context, looks like:

- Good sleep

- Protein/food throughout the day

- Not too much caffeine

- Keeping my eyes on Jesus

- Keeping a Sabbath (although Hebrews 4 tells us that we can have a Sabbath rest as a state of being; protecting downtime and intimacy with the Lord is critical)

- Wielding the Word

- Staying in a place of peace emotionally

- Being self-aware and self-controlled

While this is not a comprehensive list, I have found these keys to be very helpful for me. While I don't do these perfectly all the time, being intentional about them has helped me tremendously in growing in my gift of discernment. Another thing to keep in mind in this wisdom is not moving into legalism. I don't do well with a bunch of rules. These are just good guidelines for me. I've noticed that when I don't live this way, I can really tell emotionally and physically. My ability to discern gets blurred. I've learned through experience that staying sharp is important to me. I want to keep myself healthy and alert so I can be available no matter the circumstance. In other words, staying sharp is a choice, not a mandate.

3. Practice.

Using spiritual gifts take practice, practice, practice! Position yourself to use your gifts all the time. Yes, in the grocery store and gas station, too. It's good to start looking at using our gifts as a lifestyle, not an event.

4. Discern the beautiful

If we're wired negatively or are leaning towards hyper-spirituality, we will have a propensity to try and discern every demon in the room. Discernment is a wonderful gift that God has given us to partner with Him and to guide us through life. It is not meant to solely discern things in the demonic realm. God has a vast, beautiful, heavenly world He'd love for us to get more familiar with. The more we see heaven, the more we can release heaven.

The Gift of Discernment

When I teach the "Languages of the Spirit" series, I ask our students, "How many of you, when you were a kid, felt certain things when you got around other adults or certain environments and 'knew' they were safe and fun or, in some cases, 'knew' they were bad?" Invariably, most of the class will raise their hands. I then tell them that this is an indicator that the gift of discernment has always worked in their lives.

What many call being a "feeler" or "empath" is often just a gift of discernment. The problem is, early in life when this gift starts to operate, we may not have had language to explain what we were experiencing. To complicate matters, parents or guardians may have dismissed this behavior as being "overly-sensitive." Their response may have been, "Get over it," or "You're embarrassing the family. You will hang out with Aunt So-and-So whether you like it or not," as they yank their little discerner out of the car.

Before I go on, I realize this may strike a painful chord with some readers. It's good to understand that if our gifts have been misunderstood, many of us may have shut them down over time. And that's only natural. When gifts aren't recognized, honored, or understood, they cease to be cultivated and start to stagnate, or can carry with them much pain and confusion. I'd like to offer this prayer for you. As you read it, open your heart to receive healing and restoration:

"God, I pray that You go to the place in my heart that was either shut down by me or was ignored, mowed over, or violated by an adult (name specifically, if you can remember) and begin Your healing process. I forgive them for misunderstanding my gift or being too preoccupied to listen to my heart. I bless the gift of discernment You put in my life and I trust You to restore it in a beautiful way, in Jesus' Name. Amen."

God is restoring the gifts He's given you! He is so committed to you and greatly desires that you live in the fullness of all that Jesus purchased on the cross for you. You are going to have so much fun with all He's resurrecting in your life that you'll feel like it's Christmas!

Getting Familiar with the Gift of Discernment

The gift of discernment is basically a knowing. Have you ever caught yourself saying things like, "I just *felt* like…" or "I just seemed to *know*…" I would suggest that this type of language is giving you insight into your gift of discernment. Discernment is something that happens instinctively and intuitively. It's not a knowing that originates from logic. It's a knowing that is often referred to as "going with your gut." As you begin to become more aware of your gift, look for words in your speech like *sensed*, *felt*, *knew*, or *perceived*.

It is very important to know in this learning process that discernment is not judgment. This is also where the gift can get distorted or misunderstood. Judgment dwells in the realm of opinion, assumption, and suspicion. Often when we think we are discerning something we are really just looking at it from the viewpoint of the flesh. This is where living in the Spirit, knowing one another after the Spirit, having our minds renewed, and our senses trained is critical.

Where it can get even trickier is when those of us who are strong discerners perceive through our emotions. As emotional beings, we have to possess self-control, one of the fruits of the Spirit, to bridle our feelings so we can discern clearly. The distinction between letting our feelings dictate what we're experiencing and actually sensing what's happening in an environment can be a fine line. It's good to know that discerning through emotions is completely different than emotions dictating what we're experiencing.

You may have heard of the term "feeler." It's often used interchangeably with a discerner or intercessor. The New Age community refers to this type of person as an "empath." They're both basically the ability to discern. Have you ever gotten around a person and felt an overwhelming, yet unfamiliar feeling, such as anger? If this emotion is not one that is common for you, I'd like to suggest that you're sensing what that person is currently experiencing. That's how easy discernment can be. It's also how frustrating discernment can be if you don't know that's what you're actually doing.

This is why it is so vital to know what's going on within you before you walk into an environment. For example, if you walk into a room and are suddenly overcome with fear, but you didn't feel that way at all beforehand, you are most likely picking up the predominant spirit in the atmosphere. However, if fear is a common experience for you, it can be very hard to determine if what you're sensing is your own experience or what's happening in the room. Sometimes it's both.

Do you see how knowing what's going on *within* you is so critical to discernment? We can be tossed to and fro by the activity in an environment and not even know why. If we stay sharp, we can learn to better discern. Self-awareness plays a huge key in discernment. The more I'm aware of what's going on within me, the more I can discern what's happening outside of me.

When we are not self-aware and are overwhelmed with all sorts of anxious feelings we tend to own these experiences. We may call a friend and wail, "Pray for me! I just got hit with so much fear!!! It's an attack!" when maybe it wasn't even ours to begin with. And I would suggest it most certainly is not an attack of the enemy. We give the enemy way too much credit. We may be discerning his schemes and plans, but we're not subject to them. God gave us the ability to discern the way the enemy operates so we can dismantle those structures. God is *allowing* us to experience these things so we can take authority over them!

Often our spirits discern but our soul (mind) hasn't come into the maturity or realization that our gift is at work. This is how we can feel like we're going crazy. Imagine how people who don't yet know the Lord feel, out in the world, with a discernment sensitivity! It can definitely feel more like a curse than a gift when we don't understand it.

One time, I was walking up to a church service and got increasingly fearful. Every step I took, I was filled with more fear. I could barely handle myself as I got into the prophetic booths to minister. As we got started in our huddle up time, our overseer asked how we were all doing and I explained what was happening in my emotions. She told us that fear is often what the enemy releases to get people's focus off what Jesus is doing. We knew we were going to be imparting God's heart that night and knew how to intercede. As soon as this tactic was exposed, I immediately relaxed and all the fear left. Many of God's children felt His love that night as we released words of destiny.

This scenario can be tricky if fear is common for you. If you've had a familiar spirit of fear in your life and you walk into an environment like this, you may automatically think it's an old behavior or you are just feeling really anxious about prophesying. You may think the enemy is trying to mess you up and text all your friends that you're under attack. But this is where you need to lean into the Holy Spirit and ask, "Is this me or the environment?" This is especially important if it wasn't very clear before you arrived at the destination.

When you discern something that you know is not you, the next step is to ask the Lord how He would like you to partner with Him in what you're discerning. Ask the Holy Spirit what He wants to release in the room, what to bind up, or how to intercede (we'll go into this more in the chapter entitled, "The Honor of a King and Priest").

In the process of discernment, our spirit is the initiator of what we're sensing in a room, not our flesh. For instance, if I have offense in my heart towards someone and I walk into a room where they're seated and begin to have feelings of ill-will, I am most likely not discerning but judging based on past experience. If I walk into a room with no real negative history towards anyone and start to have feelings of ill-will, I can then ask God about it because I know it wasn't mine to begin with. Can you see how personal emotions dictating what I'm feeling *versus* discernment by the Spirit filtered through my emotions is at play in this scenario? It's a very subtle difference. A pure heart helps us use a gift of discernment without agenda. Self-awareness, the renewing of our minds, and intentionality will help us grow in this gifting, as well. Availability and alertness will aid in the learning process as we practice using this gift in partnership with the Holy Spirit.

Practice, over time, develops discernment into a mature gift. As we go through the process of soul healing, it will be easier to use the gift more intuitively because we have allowed God to heal hurting places and we cease to look at the world through a lens of woundedness. It can be very difficult to discern what's going on in the spirit when we can't even sort through our own emotions, or are so numbed out in depression we can't feel at all. God longs to heal us so we can use the gifts He's given us purely and with integrity.

Developing Maturity in Discernment

Distinguishing of spirits, or discernment, in both 1 Corinthians 12:10 and Hebrews 5:14 come from the same Greek root *diakrinō,* which, in part, means to *learn.* This gives us insight into maturing in the gift of discernment and helps us define it further. From this, we can glean some principles and keys about growing in this gift.

"To another the working of miracles; to another prophecy; to another discerning of spirits; to another divers kinds of tongues; to another the interpretation of tongues." (KJV)

1 Corinthians 12:10

"But strong meat belongeth to them that are of full age, even those who by reason of use have their senses exercised to discern both good and evil." (KJV)

Hebrews 5:14

Let's break down Hebrews 5:14 to better understand how to intentionally learn to grow in the gift of discernment. Remember, God doesn't give us gifts to confuse or torment us. He is a loving Dad who is always giving good gifts. The Bible is such an excellent resource to help us define and understand the gifts God gives.

As we can see in this verse in Hebrews, using spiritual gifts well is done by those mature in faith. God doesn't want us to remain like babies in our quest of understanding His world. A good question to ask ourselves when reading a verse like this then is, "How do I become more mature?"

Strong meat, the deeper things of God, is apprehended by maturity. This verse gives insight into *how* to grow in maturity in the things of God: the mature use their spiritual gifts by *practicing* them. The phrase "by reason of use" is translated from Strong's to mean, "a habit whether of body or mind; power acquired by custom, practice, use."[32] As you set out to learn more about your gift of discernment and other spiritual gifts, ask the Holy Spirit to show you how to practice using them. Develop a habit of using your discerner.

Surprising to some, this verse indicates that our senses are used in the process of discerning. Strange as it may sound, we can use our sense of smell, sight, sound, touch, and taste when discerning, experiencing visions, and having other spiritual encounters. We've talked a lot about using our emotions in the process of discernment, but Hebrews 5:14 tells us that our senses can be trained or exercised to help us distinguish things of the Spirit, as well.

"Senses" here is defined as the "faculty of the mind for perceiving, understanding, and judging." The root of this word is *aisthanomai* and it means, "to perceive, by the bodily senses; with the mind."[33] This reveals that we use our bodily senses and the faculties of our mind in the process of distinguishing good and evil. You might be thinking, "Wait a minute, I thought you said we don't use logic in discernment." That's true. But think of the mind in this context as a tool that helps us process, much like a computer, rather than something interjects opinion. This is why purity of thought is also so vital in the process of discernment. If we rely on our fleshly mind, discerning will be more difficult. But if we use our renewed mind, it will assist us in the process of distinguishing of spirits.

In the process of discerning, both good and evil, we can exercise our gift like we'd exercise our muscles. This is how our senses become trained. The more we intentionally use the gift, the stronger it will get. As we said in the last chapter, this word *exercised* in the Greek is the word *gymnazō* and it is most likely where we get the English word *gymnasium*. The more we work out our senses and mind to get stronger in the things of God, the greater we can operate in the gift of discernment.

Part of the maturation process, as I've previously indicated, is to shift from a fascination with the demonic realm and allow God to help us discern the good. Hebrews 5 indicates that we discern both good and evil. Discerning the good can look like an endless number of things. We can be in a church service and discern the flow of the Holy Spirit, we can discern what the angels are doing in a room, we can discern what God wants to release over a person or in a corporate environment, and we can discern the gifts in a person.

I often see a myriad of things in a corporate church environment during worship, especially when I'm tuned in. It's so much fun! One interesting thing that I've seen several times is every person's head opened up like the top of a can of soup. I know this sounds weird and maybe disgusting, but this picture is clear and is discerned with peace. I have come to know this, instinctively, as God wanting to open minds so revelation can easily be deposited. To break this experience down further and demonstrate how the gifts works together, I am discerning what God is wanting to do, through the faculty of my mind, utilizing my bodily sense of sight, and I partner with Him to release it through prophetic declaration or prophetic intercession. Typically, it's a simple prayer of acknowledgment and agreement.

God, of course, allows us to discern evil, but it's with a divine purpose. He may allow us to discern a plan or scheme of the enemy, what the enemy is trying to release in an atmosphere, the predominant spirit over a region, or what spirit is at work in someone's life. God doesn't show us these things to scare us or puff us up. He shows us what the enemy is doing so we can partner with Him to make those situations look more like heaven.

In the process of discernment, know that everything God shows us is with the purpose of partnership. He wants us to rise up in our positions of sons and daughters releasing His truth and heaven's activities into the earth.

Looking a Little More Closely

Let's take a look at examples of how our bodily senses can aid in the discernment process from different verses in the Bible.

- **Hearing** – The word "hearing" in Isaiah 6:8 is the word *shamah`* and in Revelation 1:10 is the word *akouo*. They both mean to *perceive...by ear*.[34]

- **Seeing** – Revelation 4:1 defines this word as *eido*. It means to *see* or to *perceive* with the eyes.[35]

- **Tasting** – The word *taste* in Psalm 119:103 is translated from the root word *chanak*, which means to *train* or *dedicate*.[36]

- **Smelling** – The word fragrance in 2 Corinthians 2:14 is the word *osme,* which means a *literal or figurative* smell.[37]

- **Feeling** – This word is found in Matthew 16:8. It is the word *ginosko* which means, "*to learn to know, come to know, get knowledge of, perceive, feel.*"[38]

I have heard from so many people that they think they're "making something up" when it comes to being activated in the gifts of the Spirit. I have felt that way myself at times. Learning to grow in our spiritual gifts, such as discernment, requires that we do, at first, what is counter-intuitive to us until it becomes natural. The more we operate from our new man, the more natural discerning through our new mind and bodily senses will become.

We were designed by God to be lead of our spirits, using the new mind He gave us. The soul is the place of our mind, will, and emotions. We have to learn to put off our old man and its practices and put on our new man, which is constantly being renewed in Jesus (see Colossians 3). The temptation we often struggle with is that our old man keeps wanting to get back in charge. My dad often says, "You're dead to the old man, but he isn't dead to you."

This process of maturation requires that we are aware of the reality that we do have two natures within us vying for supremacy. Living by our spirit man takes lots of practice and can be somewhat awkward at first, like learning a foreign language. It may seem uncomfortable for a while, but after time, it becomes the norm. As we continually immerse ourselves in the things of the Spirit, the things of our flesh become more evident, easier to spot, and easier to subjugate. Our spirits are meant to lead us, not our soul. Shifting our bodily senses from primarily experiencing the natural realm, then, to discerning in the Spirit takes practice but will become more and more "natural."

How Discernment Works with Other Gifts

A common mistake we can make is to think that the gifts of the Spirit operate separately from one another. This can be due to legalism or misunderstanding of how the Holy Spirit gives the gifts. As indicated in the last chapter, the Holy Spirit gives to people affectionately and prompts as the situation calls. You might be asking, "Wait, I thought you said you believed people already had these gifts." Yes, that's true. But I believe the Holy Spirit redeems the gifts and empowers people to use them for His strategic purposes. When we get saved, everything about us is redeemed for eternal significance.

Additionally, if we think that discernment is only for a select few, we may exclude ourselves from that list. If we think that only a group of chosen people are meant to prophesy, for instance, we will most likely never make ourselves available to God to speak on His behalf.

Using our gift of discernment, along with the other gifts can be quite easy. When we make ourselves available to God and begin to tune into what He's doing in any environment, we start to see the gifts work together.

For me, it looks like beginning with a prayer:

"Okay, Lord, I sense "this" in the room. How would you like me to partner with You? What do You want me to release (loose)? What do You want me to take authority over and stop (bind up), in Jesus' Name?"

God may then prompt me to go prophesy over someone and release His beautiful plans for their life. He may want me to bind up infirmity and release healing by the laying on of hands. Or He may prompt me intercede on behalf of a corporate group of people, without any outward action.

When you discern something in an atmosphere, simply ask God what He'd like you to do with what He's showing you. Often discernment is the gift that makes us *aware* of the fact that God wants to do something. Then, when we make ourselves available, He invites us to partner with Him to prophesy, heal, or perform something miraculous to change that place to look more like heaven!

A word of caution: When we sense, discern, or perceive something, we're to ask the Holy Spirit how He'd like us to partner with Him. We want to be available and we want to be lead. It can be easy to sense something in a person or a room and say, "Okay, God. I got it from here." This can be so tempting. Often, we can get comfortable in our gifts and strive to make a formula out of the process, doing what God prompted us to do that last time we ministered. Or in immaturity, be overzealous and get out ahead of what the Holy Spirit is doing next. Ironically, what the Holy Spirit may have us do with what He's showing us is completely different than what we would have assumed or drawn from past experience.

Remember, the things of the Spirit aren't often logical. Like the wind, the Holy Spirit comes and goes as He pleases.[39] Does this mean not relying on logic equals disorder? Absolutely not. This is where one of the keys from the previous chapter comes into play. The Spirit of God will not act in any way in error to the Word of God. The Bible tells us that God is not the author of confusion.[40] Doing things by the Spirit will not equal disorder or chaos. It just means it will often mess with your logical mind and propensity towards the familiar.

Discernment is like the gate, the entryway to the things of the Spirit. It is usually the gift that helps us tap in to what God is desiring for us to join Him in accomplishing in any given situation.

Know One Another After the Spirit

Another facet of discerning is to know one another after the Spirit. 2 Corinthians 5:16 says, "From now on, we are not to regard anyone after the flesh." We are not to know one another after the flesh at all. If you were to get to know me solely after the flesh, you would begin to see my shortcomings, weaknesses, and issues. But the Bible tells us to know one another after the Spirit.

Knowing one another in this capacity allows us to see each other through the eyes of Jesus. We can exercise the gifts of the Spirit and use Kingdom principles in our interactions with people because we are *choosing* to relate to them the way God instructs us to do so. Even when people can be really mean or unkind, we can choose to live in the Spirit. By doing so, we won't satisfy the desires of the flesh to lash out at them or defend ourselves. Knowing one another after the Spirit allows us to truly love unconditionally. That means, there are no conditions, no circumstances in which I won't love you.

Operating on this level eliminates interpersonal issues. It is a transcendent way of living. Not in a prideful way, but it's truly rising above personal issues and living from our new address (see Ephesians 2:6). This takes lots of practice, refining, and dying to ourselves. As we seek to know everyone after the Spirit, it becomes easier to look past shortcomings or junk and partner with God to discern how He'd like us to minister to, pray for, and interact with everyone.

Discerning Angels

Sensing what's happening in a room, for me, is often perceiving heaven's activities, not the demonic. In fact, I rarely focus on what the enemy is up to because I am more interested in partnering with God in doing what He's doing. As I'm in a corporate environment, for instance, I turn my attention to God to get pictures or impressions of what He's releasing or what angels are doing in the atmosphere.

I would like to take a moment to share some thoughts on angels. I personally don't engage with angels or initiate conversation with them. The Lord has not given me a revelation to this end. When I sense what angels are doing, I communicate with the Holy Spirit by acknowledging the angelic activity and partnering with Him in what I sense He's doing through them. Depending on the scenario, my prayer may look like, "God, thank You for sending Your messengers today. I sense they are releasing creativity in the room. I agree with You that You are doing a new thing and I partner with You to release a renaissance in the church through creativity and color."

I have a conviction that I am only to engage with the Holy Spirit. He is my Guide, my go-to, and my go-through. In Psalm 91:11, it says that God will command His angels concerning our needs, not that I command His angels. With Daniel and Zechariah, for instance, we get further insight. An angel of the Lord appeared to them. Yet, the angels were not summoned. Although both these men had extensive conversations with angels, the angels were doing the instructing and informing, not vice versa. Additionally, when Jesus finished 40 days of testing in the wilderness, angels came and ministered to Him. But we don't see a record of Jesus, as a man, telling the angels what to do. They were sent by the Father to attend to His needs.

Do I think there may be exceptions to this? Yes, absolutely. God wants us to follow the Holy Spirit's lead, not create rigid rules. However, if we look at the bulk of Scripture, this is not the norm.

I believe that anything angelic inspires awe and wonder. I mean, who doesn't want to see a 25-foot angel in the room!? But God knows our inclination to get our eyes off Jesus. As we see with John the Revelator, humans are prone to worshipping angels. And angels don't like that. They spend time with Jesus. They see His beauty and glory and know all that He's done for humanity. They know that Jesus is the only One to be worshipped. There are angels, in fact, whose only job is to worship Him 24/7 for all of eternity (see Revelation 4)!

We get further insight through the Word on the topic of human-angel interaction:

"I, John, am the one who heard and saw these things. When I heard and saw them, I fell down to worship at the feet of the angel who had shown them to me. But he said to me, "Don't do that! I am a fellow slave with you, your brothers the prophets, and those who keep the words of this book. Worship God!"

Revelation 22:8-9

"Do not let anyone who delights in false humility and the worship of angels disqualify you. Such a person also goes into great detail about what they have seen; they are puffed up with idle notions by their unspiritual mind." (NIV)

Colossians 2:18

We can draw from these verses that angels don't like to be worshipped and they aren't to be worshipped. Man has a propensity to adore and admire whatever is awe-inspiring. Additionally, we see that angel worship can lead to, among other things, false humility. False humility is a form of pride and can cause us to get caught up in mystical experiences that take our focus off Jesus.

God knows our weaknesses. He knows that we are susceptible to pride. His Word gives us all the instruction we need to be protected, even from ourselves!

With all that being said, when I do perceive angels in a room, I pay attention. I observe what they're doing. I usually do get a sense of what they are there for. However, I still make a point of asking the Lord how He'd like me to partner with Him in what *He's* doing. Sometimes I just watch the angels (with my spirit eyes) to see how they're behaving so I can continue to learn.

The word *angel* literally means messenger,[41] so when they come into an environment or are perceived, we can know, by definition, they are there with an assignment or message from God! They come with gifts from God's heart to change any and every situation to look more like heaven. In fact, every good thing comes down from our Papa who loves to delight us with good gifts (see James 1:17).

One time, in a church service during worship, I saw a briefcase open and a bunch of angels pour out into the congregation. I thanked God for what He was doing in the atmosphere and agreed with Him that He was releasing heaven's activities into the room. I knew people would be getting messages, downloads, and ideas from God. I blessed His heart to equip and inspire people.

Another time, I was in a room teaching. It was one of the most difficult seasons of my life. I was in a crucible. I could, and perhaps will, write a book on the purpose of this season. It was very intense. Needless to say, I was close to giving up. I felt as if I was being pressed in on all sides and if it wasn't for the grace of God, would have abandoned what He was preparing me for and calling me to. On this particular night, the pain and frustration had mounted so greatly that I didn't know how I could carry on with the teaching. As I was sitting up in front of the class, I sensed an angel about ten feet away from me in the center aisle. I couldn't really see his face. He was holding a clip board, watching me, and taking notes. It was fascinating. I wasn't getting any feelings from or towards him, negative or positive. It was a very neutral experience. He watched me and made notations, as I watched him observing me. I knew instinctively that he was there to report back to the Lord on my behavior. He was there to answer some important questions about my choice of free will: "What will she do when everyone rejects her? How will she behave? What choice will she make in the face of resistance?" This was a sobering moment. It also gave me better awareness and understanding of the great cloud of witnesses that are cheering us on. All of heaven, in fact, waits with anticipation to see whether we will make choices to satisfy this temporal existence or those of eternal consequence.

I've had many conversations with God about why I can see demons with my natural eyes but not angels. It's quite frustrating. However, I believe this is for two reasons. One, knowing that I'm prone to pride, God is protecting me from getting too fascinated with angels. Two, the demonic loves attention. It works overtime to distract us from what God's doing. Conversely, angels want to point us to Jesus. They don't want to be the center of attention.

If you have a passion or pull on your heart to learn more about the spirit realm, I would encourage you to ask the Holy Spirit to lead you in this process and use the Word as a rudder to guide you in your learning journey.

Personal Examples of Discernment

- Sometimes God will help me know who to prophesy over by pointing out a person who reminds me of someone else, or it seems to be someone that I've met before. One day I was walking down the hallway at church and I met two guys who were with one of our pastors. Immediately, I asked one of the guys if we'd met before. He said that we hadn't and I knew that God had a word for him. I asked him if I could prophesy over him and release what I was sensing God was saying about his life.

- Another facet of discernment for me is feeling God's heart for a person. When I prophesy over people, sometimes I get so overwhelmed with love for them and I know that I'm discerning God's heart towards them. It is so wonderful! From this place of discernment, I prophesy His heart.

- One time, I was in a church service and I started to get immense pains in my chest. It was so painful, I was worried I was dying. I couldn't breathe, my chest was constricting, and I began to panic. I went to the back of the room and asked a pastor to pray with me. As she was praying, another pastor from the front of the room called out a word of knowledge about a spirit of death, accompanied by chest pains and shortness of breath. He commanded a spirit of suicide to leave. Immediately, my symptoms left. I learned that I was discerning in my physical body what was going on in the room. Now I know that when these sorts of things happen I can take authority over them, in Jesus' Name, and release His peace. This level of learning had to come through practice and intentionality. Had I thought the physical pain was my own issue or relegated it to an attack of the enemy, I would have never learned more about my gift of discernment.

- In Acts 16:16, Paul and Silas were going to pray and a slave girl, who had a spirit of divination that enabled her to "predict" the future, followed them yelling, "These men are servants of the Most High God! These men are servants of the Most High God!" And she kept doing this for many days. The Bible says that, finally, Paul was *aggravated* and commanded the spirit to leave. It left that instant. Have you ever approached someone or been in a situation and grown increasingly irritated? True, it may just be impatience or too much coffee. But I would propose to you that you may also be discerning a spirit at work. Although what this girl was saying was true, she was operating under the power of a negative spirit. An indication that you're discerning something can be demonstrated by an aggravation such as this. I remember I was in a church service one time during worship and two guys were talking in the back of the room. Now, usually, these sorts of things don't bother me because I am used to people giving or receiving ministry to one another during worship. But this time was different. As they continued to talk, I continued to grow more and more agitated. I was in a volunteer leadership position so I knew I had the authority to ask them to stop. I approached them and one guy, who was doing most of the talking, snapped at me and said he was telling the other guy about Jesus. "What's wrong with that!?" he said. I thanked and affirmed him but asked if they would kindly step into the lobby, because it was presenting a distraction for other people. They stormed off. I would suggest to you that I was discerning either a spirit of distraction or a fleshly drivenness by this man, probably rooted rejection and in a need for significance.

- When our son was just a baby, I would often fall asleep with him on my chest out of sheer exhaustion. This one night we fell asleep with the TV on. As we were sleeping, something really uncomfortable roused me awake. I was very unsettled in my emotions, just short of scared. One might call this the "willies." I woke up to find a ghost hunter show had just started on the same channel that I had fallen asleep to during a house remodel show. As I processed what was happening, I knew that I could sense (discern) in my spirit, while I was asleep, that the ghost show was releasing something negative into our home. I turned it off and the feeling went away.

- It can be easy to pick up on what music artists are going through by listening to their lyrics. It's the same with a preacher or poet. One time I was listening to a new artist and, although the subject matter of the song was one of despair, I sensed this overwhelming current of hope that the artist himself carried. I perceived a heart of compassion and justice from this person. When this happens to me, I bless this person's God-given gifts, release encounters with Him over their life, and acknowledge that God created them for a special, eternal purpose.

Reflection

1. Think back on your childhood. What experiences have you had in which you just "knew" things or "felt" things about certain people, environments, or situations? Write them down. Be specific. Ask Holy Spirit to help you.

_____

_____

2. Growing up, in what ways have you felt "misunderstood?" How could this be connected to a spiritual gift?

_____

_____

3. In what ways do you already know that you have spiritual sensitivities (i.e. awareness of spiritual things like angels, demons, or the manifest Presence of God, etc.)?

_____

_____

Activation

Activation #1

Go into a corporate environment, like a church service, and be intentional about using your gift of discernment. Use the notepad on your phone or bring your journal and write down everything that you sense, feel, or perceive. Talk with the Holy Spirit about it. If you bring a friend with you, compare notes after service.

Activation #2

Look up a few worship and secular songs and listen to them. Ask the Holy Spirit to help you choose which songs. Close your eyes as you listen to each one and write down what impressions, feelings, or things you sense about the song, lyrics, melody, or band.

Activation #3

Ask the Lord to teach you how to use your senses and mind to discern and understand spiritual things. Write down what He speaks to your heart. Then, make a practice of engaging with Him through what He shows you.

Prophecy

"For you can all prophesy one by one, so that everyone may learn and everyone may be encouraged...Therefore, my brothers, be eager to prophesy ..."
1 Corinthians 14:31, 39

Debunking myths and misconceptions is so much fun. I am so grateful to the teachers in my life who have brought new paradigms to previous old wineskin understandings. Jesus tells us that we can't experience the new thing He has for us if we have old wineskins. Nor, would we take brand new cloth and sew it onto an old pair of jeans to patch a hole. As soon as we wash it, the new material will surely shrink and pull away from the old material.[42] Through these parables, Jesus is saying that we have to get rid of old belief systems and structures within our minds in order for new revelation to have fertile ground in our hearts.

One paradigm that is really starting to shift in the Body of Christ is that of prophecy. Not only is the gift itself starting to be rightly understood and used within the New Testament context and definition, but we are starting to embrace the reality that God wants us *all* to prophesy and that the Bible, in fact, says we all can.

Some of the material in this chapter may be review for you or it may be completely new. Wherever you are on the spectrum of understanding prophecy, I'm confident the Holy Spirit will speak something new to you about the gift of prophecy. Remember, as you read, use the Holy Spirit Highlights page in the back of the manual to write down things that jump out at you so you can explore them later with the Lord.

If you've been in the church for any period of time you've received or, no doubt, heard someone else receive a bad prophecy. This "prophetic" word was shaming, exposing, confusing, or accusing. You or the other recipient most likely left feeling discouraged, condemned, or embarrassed.

You probably know where I'm going with this, but this word was NOT from God and is not Biblically sound. You might be thinking, "Well, how can you say that if you weren't there?" I can confidently tell you this was not from God because it was not an accurate reflection of His heart. God is love and everything He thinks and does towards us is of encouragement and kindness. Additionally, this word did not follow the New Testament guidelines for prophecy so, therefore, it is not aligned with the Word of God.

In this chapter, we are going to learn more about the gift of prophecy and why the Bible tells us that we can all function in this gift.

Offices and Gifts[43]

Before we break down the gift of prophecy, we'll define the role of a prophet and look at the difference between the two.

The office of prophet, like the other offices in the five-fold ministry, is a call by God. Let's take a peek at a couple passages that give us insight into the office of prophet.

"And He personally gave some to be apostles, some prophets, some evangelists, some pastors and teachers, for the training of the saints in the work of ministry, to build up the body of Christ, until we all reach unity in the faith and in the knowledge of God's Son, growing into a mature man with a stature measured by Christ's fullness. Then we will no longer be little children, tossed by the

waves and blown around by every wind of teaching, by human cunning with cleverness in the techniques of deceit. But speaking the truth in love, let us grow in every way into Him who is the head—Christ. From Him the whole body, fitted and knit together by every supporting ligament, promotes the growth of the body for building up itself in love by the proper working of each individual part."

Ephesians 4:11 – 16

From this passage in Ephesians, we see that Jesus Himself is the One who appoints apostles, prophets, evangelists, pastors, and teachers to a position called an "office." People don't self-appoint and these offices come with specific responsibilities. Some of these duties include: training and equipping the Body of Christ, helping the Body get to a place of maturity, rightly handling and instructing in the Word (and I would suggest inspiring the Body to get into the Word themselves), teaching the Body to grow in discernment, administering loving correction and discipline, and exampling love as a lifestyle.

We get more insight into this office from the first chapter of Jeremiah:

"The word of the Lord came to me:
I chose you before I formed you in the womb;
I set you apart before you were born.
I appointed you a prophet to the nations.
But I protested, "Oh no, Lord, God! Look, I don't know how to speak since I am only a youth."
Then the Lord said to me:
Do not say, "I am only a youth,"
for you will go to everyone I send you to
and speak whatever I tell you.
Do not be afraid of anyone,
for I will be with you to deliver you.
This is the Lord's declaration.
Then the Lord reached out His hand, touched my mouth, and told me:
I have now filled your mouth with My words.
See, I have appointed you today
over nations and kingdoms
to uproot and tear down,
to destroy and demolish,
to build and plant."

Jeremiah 1:4-10

I love this passage for many reasons! We can draw so many things from these verses about God's heart: He sets people up for success, He's always working in advance for His purposes, and He qualifies people for what He calls them to. Although not everyone in the Body of Christ is called to an office, we can see principles for us in this passage of Scripture.

In verse four, God tells Jeremiah that *before* he was even born, He had an awesome plan for Jeremiah's life. God marked Jeremiah with a divine design! Jeremiah didn't decide one day what he wanted his call to be, he got an invitation from God. This passage is key to helping us understand a selection to office of prophet. Being called to an office is by appointment. There are some in the Body of Christ putting the title "Prophet" or "Apostle" before their name that God has never appointed. I would suggest this may have to do with a need for significance or recognition. Our job is not to call anyone out because we don't know whom God has or hasn't called. We need to honor everyone. But it's vital for us to understand that we do not self-appoint. We can certainly all desire to prophesy, but we aren't all called to the office of prophet.

When God spoke to Jeremiah, Jeremiah's immediate thoughts were negative. He argued with God and made an attempt to disqualify himself based on age and, perhaps, lack of command of the language or knowledge of Scripture. God called Jeremiah. But Jeremiah contended with Him (in my own words), "Are you crazy or something!? I'm just a kid. I can't do this." God responded by saying, "Don't disqualify yourself. I'll put My words and plans within you. I will empower you to do what I've called you to do. All you have to do is say 'yes.'" Ironically, it's often people whom God calls that want to shy away from the title and function. Sometimes when people are called by God to an office and they realize the call is great, they will attempt to dismiss the invitation because of perceived inability. And that's right where God wants them.

In fact, it's in weakness that God can move through people more powerfully. In 2 Corinthians 12, Paul had an issue that was tormenting him. He pleaded with God to take it away, but God said, "My grace is sufficient for you, for My power is made perfect in weakness." We can relax! We don't have to strive for qualification for any office or gift. When we feel weak, God says His power is actually perfected in us! Small caution here; as indicated in the last chapter, I am not talking about the lowly-worm doctrine that teaches us that we're all just dirt and sinners. I could write a whole book on that alone! There are certainly some paradoxes in the Christian life, but humility and surrender are not synonymous with groveling.

"Paul, called as an apostle of Christ Jesus by God's will…"

1 Corinthians 1:1

Paul is another beautiful example of someone you'd probably never guess to be called of God to such a key position in the Body of Christ. Paul ordered the killings of the very people he was called to (although he didn't yet know it)! One thing he did know, after his encounter with God on the road to Damascus, he was called by the same Jesus he was persecuting. God loves to use the most unsuspecting, you'd-never-nominate-or-guess-in-a-million-years people.

As with the gift of prophecy, however, I do believe we can all, to some extent, have apostolic giftings. The word *apostolos* means "one sent forth with orders."[44] When we are equipped and sent by an apostolic leader or covering to go out and change the world we are functioning in an apostolic-type capacity. Does this mean we are all apostles? No. But, again, Isaiah 9:7 says, "Of the increase of His government and peace there will be no end." (NKJV) We could use Kingdom as another word for government here. When Jesus said, "Your Kingdom come, Your will be done, on earth as it is in heaven," He was giving us a model prayer to pray. So, although we are not all apostles, we are all responsible to extend the Kingdom wherever we go!

In looking at the office of prophet from a different angle, I'd like to propose a scenario. At the time of this writing, there are just over seven billion people in the world. Reportedly, there are just over two billion Christians. That's just about 30% of the world's population.

Out of the two billion Christians on the planet, what percentage of this Christian population do you think is called to an office? Can you imagine if 75% of Christians were called to one of the five offices in the Church? If this were the case, who would go out into the world to change all realms of society from the inside out? If we were all called to equip the Body as our full-time job, there wouldn't be many Christians left to infiltrate the spheres of influence in the world of government, business, education, arts and entertainment, family, sports, media, science, technology, healthcare, etc.[45]

Now, it's true that I actually don't know how many Christians are called to an office. But we can deduce that if we, being all different members of one Body, have different functions, I would suggest that many of us are called to extend the Kingdom right where we're at in our cubicles, surgery rooms, business conventions, classrooms, and the restaurants where we're waiting tables.

The office of prophet is a position appointed by God to equip the Body of Christ with supernatural weapons and wisdom to thwart the plans of hell and release the Kingdom of God. I do believe people called to the five-fold ministry can influence and advise people within the other spheres beyond the church, especially having access to and influence with high-level people like presidents, military leaders, CEOs and the like. But someone called to a five-fold office position has a primary function to equip people in the Body of Christ to go out and change the world.

The Gift of Prophecy

Prophecy is a gift given to people by the Holy Spirit to come alongside their other giftings and to complement their unique destiny. Prophecy is not something that requires any type of qualification. The gift can definitely be refined and strengthened, but we don't have to perform for it. Like Jeremiah, we don't want to disqualify ourselves from using the gift. The Holy Spirit affectionately gives this gift to us because it is so important to God. And we'll see why in this chapter.

Many people have been hurt by the misuse of the gift of prophecy. I'm sure you're aware of a familiar scenario: A speaker on stage with a microphone calls a person out of the congregation, asks them to stand up, and then proceeds to identify the sin in that person's life, warning that they better get right with the Lord or else. I've unfortunately seen this scenario just recently.

If we talk about the "why's" surrounding the abuse of this gift, we can discover a host of reasons. But I truly believe that the people who misuse prophecy just haven't had encounters with God's love that have truly penetrated their hearts. The more we are transformed by God's love, the more we desire and are able to properly represent Him. The less that we've had a true encounter with Him, we filter our gifts and His Word through opinions, wounds, and agenda.

Some people hold to an Old Testament style of prophecy, completely overlooking the fact that Jesus ushered in a New Covenant and made a way for man to have a direct relationship with God. Because the Israelites demanded that Moses, for instance, hear from God on their behalf and insisted on having kings rule over them instead of having an intimate relationship with God themselves, God used kings, priests, and prophets to communicate to them and rule over them.

New Covenant, New Way to Prophesy

God often asked Old Testament prophets to warn Israel of their actions and impending consequences. If Israel continued in their sin of idolatry, for instance, God would turn them over to the works of their own hands, bondage. It was the result of sowing and reaping. In reading through the Old Testament, however, I've seen God's heart of love and incredible patience with this "stiff-necked," stubborn people. God always draws us, as He did Israel, with love (the book of Hosea wrecks me every time I read it).

In the New Testament, Jesus came to fulfill the law and the prophets. He made a way for man to connect directly with God, restoring the relationship God always wanted, and ushered in a law higher than sowing and reaping. He ushered in grace. With this grace, we can now come boldly to the throne knowing that our sins and transgressions are covered in the blood of Jesus. Now that grace transcends the law, Jesus says there is only one new command for us to live by: love.[46] Freely we have received, freely we are to give.[47] His grace exemplifies the good news and His love covers a multitude of sins.

This is why it's imperative that we prophesy from a heart of love and not of consequence. Jesus gave His life as payment for sin. Now, we have the responsibility of rightly presenting the truth of love and grace that is afforded every person because of His sacrifice. He died so people could know how much they're loved. 1 Corinthians 14:1 says, "Pursue love and desire spiritual gifts, and above all that you may prophesy." Love, therefore, is to embody the gift of prophecy and use of any spiritual gift. Prophecy must be delivered through a heart of love.

I believe one of the reasons prophecy was singled out in the above verse is because we have the power of life and death in our tongues (Proverbs 18:21). If we prophesy with an Old Testament paradigm we could be speaking death into the lives of people who desperately need life! As we read in 1 Corinthians 13, love is the foundation. We are nothing if we don't prophesy in love. Prophecy rightly filtered through a heart of love builds up, it doesn't tear down (1 Corinthians 14:4). And sometimes the only way the world will see God's great love for them is through us.

Prophecy Has a Purpose

As we saw in chapter two, "Laying the Foundation," prophecy is defined as "a discourse emanating from divine inspiration and declaring the purposes of God...comforting the afflicted, or revealing things hidden; esp. by foretelling future events." In other words, prophecy is God communicating His heart to us and through us for any given situation.

1. Prophecy is a communication initiated by God.

Prophecy comes from the heart of God. When we prophesy, we are not drumming something up on our own. It takes practice to make ourselves available to God. Once we set out to discover and use the gift of prophecy, we delight in sharing what's on God's heart for a person, family, or corporate body. As we're learning to use this gift, we might be afraid that we're making something up, but God loves the fact that we're positioning our hearts to be available! As we get more experienced in what we're hearing or seeing from Him, we can be certain that we are declaring His purposes as we discern that it's coming from a heart of love. The more we practice, the more comfortable and astute we become in hearing from Him and speaking for Him.

2. Prophecy declares the purposes of God.

In Jeremiah 29:11 God says, "For I know the plans I have for you," declares the Lord, "plans to prosper you and not to harm you, plans to give you hope and a future." (NIV) The plans and purposes of God are always good, they are always to prosper us, they are not to harm, shame, or frustrate us. They are designed to give us hope and a promise for an amazing future. Nothing God does is insignificant, half-way, or deceitful. He is very intentional and loving in all that He does for us. He is full of integrity. When we partner with Him to declare His purposes through prophecy, our language will always reflect these truths.

3. Prophecy reveals hidden things, especially by foretelling future events.

God knows the future because He lives outside of time. Those of us who choose to partner with Him will be invited into mysteries that can't be accessed any other way than through Him. When we prophesy, we often share with the hearer future things and events that aren't yet their present reality, because God knows their future. Disclosing future events connects people to destiny. They may not even be aware of the plans and purposes of God for their life, but the prophetic impregnates them with promise.

Things that are hidden can be things about the Kingdom or gifts and talents that lie dormant within a person that prophecy calls to life. As an example, I saw a woman in church one day and then the Lord said to me "book." I knew that there was a gift of writing within her. I released a prophetic word about writing books and she told me that she was in the process of writing one! She was so encouraged (as was I). If you recall, from chapter one, this was also a word of knowledge packaged within a prophetic word about the completion of the book that God had placed within her.

Prophecy Has By-Products

Healthy, loving prophecy will always have certain *by-products,* as seen in 1 Corinthians 14:3. A good litmus test for a word that follows New Testament guidelines is revealed in this verse:

> *"But the person who prophesies speaks to people for edification, encouragement, and consolation..."*

> *1 Corinthians 14:3*

1. Edification

Edifying is the act of building someone up. If you look at the original root of this word, it suggests that it's like building a house.[48] When we prophesy, according to the New Testament definition, we help build people up into the man or woman God has intended them to be.

2. Encouragement

Encouragement, or exhortation, means to call near.[49] When we prophesy from God's heart of love, His words through us will cause people to draw closer to Him, they won't push people away. An example of a word like this might be, "God is so proud of you and is not disappointed in you. He's got amazing plans for your life." While this may seem like a simple word, its effects can be very profound for someone who may think God is distant, angry, or waiting to strike them with a lightning bolt. God's heart is that all His children are restored to Him and live in the fullness of what He's purposed for them.

3. Comfort

Comfort, or consolation, is meant to persuade, calm, or console.[50] When people have made a mess of their lives, have little hope, or have just received news of something personally devastating, the words of God through prophecy serve to comfort their hurting hearts. An example of a comforting word might be something like this, "Do not despair. Your season may be heavy right now but the Lord is bringing you strength today to endure so you have the ability to walk through this into the fullness of your destiny."

The Components

Now that we've looked at the definition of prophecy and the purpose of the prophetic, let's delve a little further into the prophetic word.

A prophetic word has three components:

1. Delivery

First, the Lord delivers the word. He can do this in two ways. A person can receive a word directly from God by divine download (sometimes you can identify a word directly from God by what you've journaled in your times with Him or while you're reading the Bible). However, since God loves to partner with us, He will often look for someone to deliver a word from His heart, and this is where prophecy comes in through a giver.

2. Interpretation

The interpretation of the word can sometimes accompany the delivery as we, the giver, are hearing from God and get clarification or more detail as we speak. Sometimes, the interpretation doesn't come to us as we deliver the word at all. And that's ok. I would much rather prophesy to someone one word and tell them that's all I got, than to try to force an interpretation of what I think it means. If the Lord doesn't give me any more insight, I end the word when I stop receiving. Sometimes, the interpretation is meant to come to the hearer (the one receiving the word) by the Holy Spirit so He can continue to build relationship and intimacy with them. I've found that many times when we give prophetic words, they are often a confirmation of what God has already been speaking to the hearer's heart anyway. Additionally, sometimes the interpretation is a very personal process.

3. Receiving

The last part is receiving. As we deliver the prophetic word to the recipient they are the ones to receive and steward the word. Sometimes, the word itself won't be clear right away and will take some time to come to pass. I remember a student of ours a few years ago got a word 30 years prior and it was just coming to pass and becoming fully understood that year! Another component of the receiving process is application. As the giver, we are not responsible for the application of the word. That moves into counseling or presumption, neither of which are part of prophecy. What the hearer does with the application of the word is up to them and God.

How a Prophetic Word is Received from the Lord

We can take cues from Biblical prophets on how a prophetic word is received from the Lord. God is not limited by any means to deliver a message to us (He's even used a donkey).[51] There are some main ways that we can connect with what He's saying and doing to develop and deliver a prophetic word. You'll notice that some items in the list below are the same as what we covered in the chapter on discernment. Remember that God uses many different avenues to communicate with us because He wants us to know what He's saying and He especially loves to use a native language that we're very familiar with to aid in this communication.

1. Seeing

In Jeremiah 1:11, after calling him as a prophet, the Lord says, "What do you see?" The word *see* here is the Hebrew word *ra'ah*, which means "to see, look at, inspect, perceive, consider."[52] Additional definition of the word means: "to see, perceive, to have vision, regard, look after, see after, learn about, observe, watch look upon, look out, find out, consider, give attention to, discern, distinguish, look at, gaze at."[53]

This type of seeing can either be an open vision or a vision in your mind. An open vision is a vision that you have with your natural eyes. Images in this vision are transposed on top of natural things. I remember one night I was awoken to an open vision on my ceiling. A big spotlight appeared and images moved around in the light. I woke my husband up to make sure I wasn't making it up. I asked him if he could see it. He said no. I asked him if I was really awake and he, grumpily, said yes (it was about 3:00 a.m.). I saw this vision on the ceiling with my eyes but my husband couldn't.

Most of what I get from the Lord is seeing with my mind's eye. I believe a vision or picture in our mind requires a little more faith, attention, and intimacy with the Lord because we have to develop the ability and understanding of knowing that we're experiencing a vision. In the definition above, seeing in your mind's eye is like perceiving. This is where we trust that when the

Bible says we have the mind of Christ,[54] that we become confident we're using it. Additionally, discernment aids in experiencing these types of visions. A good way to know if your experiencing one of these visions is when images pop up that you would typically never think of. For instance, recently I've been seeing a white turnip cross my mind in the Spirit during worship.

2. Hearing

In Isaiah 6:8, Isaiah says, "Then I heard the voice of the Lord saying: Who should I send? Who will go for Us?" Here the word *heard* in this passage is the Hebrew word *shama`*, which means "to hear, listen to, obey, to hear as perceived by ear, to hear of or concerning, to hear (have power to hear), to hear with attention or interest, listen to, to understand (language)."[55]

In the last chapter, we learned that often discerning can come through our bodily senses. This is where we begin to realize that our natural hearing can aid in and have a correlation to our spiritual hearing. Have you ever told someone that you "heard" the Lord say something to you, but you know that you didn't audibly hear it? I would suggest that because you hear with your natural ears, you know what the act of listening is like. So, when God speaks to your heart through this kind of conversation, you are perceiving with your spirit ears.

When we are hearing from God, sometimes this hearing can be sounds, words, phrases, or sentences. One day, I was thinking about my good friend and I heard the Lord say a phrase, "Swing for the fences." I had no idea what that meant (I didn't have the interpretation, just delivery of the word). I texted her and she was blown away! She told me she had been talking with the Lord about a deep desire of hers to speak at Harvard. She told me she thought the dream was way too big and was tempted to dismiss it. Even if a word or phrase makes no sense to you, it will often make sense to the hearer. The funny thing about this word is that my friend was a softball player through college. God not only spoke to the desire in her heart, but He was speaking *her* language!

3. Perceiving/Say In One's Heart

In Jeremiah 2:1 it says, "The word of the Lord came to me: 'Go and announce directly to Jerusalem that this is what the Lord says...'" Here the word *came* is *'amar*, which means "to say, speak, utter." The implication of this word is that it was spoken by God and perceived by Jeremiah. Additional definition means "to say, to answer, to say in one's heart, to think, to command, to promise, to intend."[56] Have you ever had something just pop into your heart or just get a "random" thought? This is what I often refer to simply as "perceiving."

This type of prophetic word from the Lord can come to a person through an internal word or inspired thought. I had an amazing experience one time when I was hanging out with the Lord where it felt like a word was literally bubbling up from my spirit, with almost a physical sensation. This type of word requires that we are very still. If we are clamorous in our emotions or mind, it's harder to perceive what God's saying. Discernment also plays a part in that it helps in your "knower" that a word is from the Lord. It's as if something leaps within you.

4. Feeling

Sometimes I can feel God's heart for someone. This happened actually happened at a Starbucks when I was working on this manual. I saw a young man at a table with someone and I felt God's heart of love and excitement over him. After a while, I went over and asked if I could share what I was getting from the Lord. As I began to tell him what I was feeling from the Lord, a prophetic word started to flow. He kept saying, "Ah, for real? For real?" with the biggest smile on his face. It was so much fun as I began to prophesy God's approval and communicate His heart for this young man's future.

5. Scripture

Receiving a prophetic word for someone from Scripture is one of the most profound ways to prophesy. Usually this will come through "hearing" or "perceiving." You may get a Scripture address and know it's for a particular person or situation. I actually believe this is one of the most significant and true ways to get a word to someone because we really don't have to weigh Scripture like we would a word filtered through human lenses. The Bible is the inspired Word of God and it can provide a real, tangible anchor for people to hang onto during a storm or provide hope through seasons of uncertainty. Does this mean that Scripture can't be misused? Of course not. But giving someone a word from Jeremiah 29:11, for instance, doesn't need much interpretation or judging and can provide all the hope a person needs to continue on in the face of adversity.

6. Dreams

God speaks to us through dreams at night. As we'll see in the chapter on dreams and dream interpretation, there is Biblical precedent for God using dreams to give prophetic direction and insight to people. Since dreams tend to be a little obscure at times and often involve much symbolism and personalization, it takes a lot of practice in hearing from the Lord to understand and correctly apply this language. I have one particular friend, however, who gives me profound, timely, and spot-on prophetic words from her dreams.

Developing the Prophetic Word

In this section, we are going to learn some guidelines and tips that will help us develop a prophetic word for someone.

Developing or crafting a prophetic word is *putting language* to what you see, perceive, hear, etc. Understanding symbolism and metaphor plays a big part in knowing what the Lord is showing you. As you develop your own dictionary with the Lord, you will find that understanding what He's saying becomes more automatic.

When prophesying, you can use these guidelines:

1. Go with your gut.

I've often found that if I "go with my gut" it's the Holy Spirit speaking to me. It's not second, third, or 18th guessing. Remember, discernment plays a part in prophesying, so going with our instincts is often our spirits knowing what the Holy Spirit is saying immediately. When logic tries to sound an alarm, we start to get confused or anxious. Go with your gut!

2. Ask Holy Spirit.

He has all the answers you need. When you get a picture, impression, feeling, etc., ask Him about it. He may surprise you and tell you something that you never would have guessed.

3. Think outside the box.

Sometimes God will use a play on words or give us creative meanings for things that we wouldn't have thought of. If you hear the word "dawn," for instance, He could be talking to you about a person named Dawn or the dawn of a new day.

4. Watch your use of Christian terms.

This is really important when you're prophesying over people in the marketplace or out in the world. They don't know a lot of Christian terms and we don't want to make it hard for them to get the message God is trying to convey by using a lot of Biblical words. Paul said he became all things to all men in order that he might save some.[57] I often find that when I'm prophesying, depending on the person or occasion, my language will change up to fit the situation. It's good to learn how to communicate spiritual things in non-religious ways to people who may not have an understanding of them.

5. Start the word with a softening statement.

Years ago, I was taught that it can be helpful to say, "I *sense* the Lord is saying...," or "I *feel* the Lord is saying..." I teach our students this approach, as well, because it lets the hearer know that God Himself may not be saying every word they're speaking and it takes the pressure off the student to get it all right all the time. This also helps the hearer not feel handcuffed to the word. If we say "The Lord says" often within a word, it can be hard for someone to evaluate the word. They may think, "Well, if God said it, who am I to judge it?" Our goal is to speak like we are the oracles of God,[58] true, but as we're learning to craft our words it is helpful to package them with grace, both for the giver and the receiver.

7.   Draw from your dictionary.

As you develop your dictionary with the Lord, you will become more adept at defining and understanding metaphoric and symbolic language. When you see pictures and visions you'll begin to instinctively know what they mean. As mentioned in chapter one, there are some great guidelines. It's helpful, for instance, to use the rule of first mention in the Bible, but we don't want to become handcuffed by it. The Holy Spirit is far too creative and far too free to be limited. Additionally, you won't find modern symbols in the Bible, like cell phones or satellite dishes. The only caveat to building your dictionary is not solely relying on it. You constantly want to be in communication with the Holy Spirit in the event He's saying something new.

8. Even if it doesn't make sense...

As I mentioned earlier in the example with my friend where the Lord said, "Swing for the fences," don't be surprised if you get words, analogies, symbolism, metaphors, language that you don't understand. Share them anyway! God likes to speak our language. He personalizes the way He talks to each one of us. Chances are the person you're prophesying over will understand what you're sharing. You may not understand the language in which He's speaking, but they certainly will!

9. Practice.

Practice, practice, practice! The only way to learn to ride a bike is to practice until you get the hang of it. It's the same with the prophetic. The more you practice, the more comfortable you'll become. You will get over the apprehension of sharing with people, you will come to understand the symbols or metaphors God uses, and you will become more certain in knowing when God is prompting you in the Spirit to prophesy.

10. Get feedback.

Another great way to grow in the prophetic is to get feedback from people. If the information provided to you is constructive and you apply what they share, you can fine tune your delivery and speech.

Evaluating the Prophetic Word

Did you know that you don't have to receive every prophetic word spoken over you? I know this may sound so obvious. But, to this day, I still struggle with some words spoken over me...until I realize I don't have to receive them all. Additionally, we want people to have the freedom to receive or reject the words we speak over them.

"Two or three prophets should speak, and the others should evaluate."

1 Corinthians 14:29

As mentioned in the chapter entitled "Laying the Foundation," the word *evaluate* here is the Greek word *diakrinō*. It's where we get the word *discern*. So, we can take away from this verse that an environment of learning, constructive input, and encouragement is in harmony with prophesying. When we tell people we are open to feedback, for instance, it allows them to have the freedom to evaluate the word we've just given them. Evaluating should be a part of the prophetic process. The reason we evaluate is to set a precedent that feedback is welcomed and to communicate that we're all just humans practicing together.

Additionally, we never want people to feel as if they have no say in whether they can receive or reject a word. Sometimes, as we're learning to prophesy (or if we have an agenda like the need for significance) we can project other things into the word. We want to empower people to weigh our words so we can all learn. Having a heart position of humility in delivery and receiving aids us in the learning process.

Tips for Evaluating

1. There is no fear in love.

God will never give you a word that makes you feel condemned, fearful, or shamed. The Bible says that love covers.[59] God is Love. So, a word from Him will never make you feel exposed or afraid. 1 Corinthians 13:7 says that love always protects. (NIV) God's heart is to protect you, not hurt you. As the giver of the word, we are to convey His heart of love, as well. Giving a prophetic word for the Lord carries with it great responsibility.

2. The Bible tells us to.

The Bible tells us to evaluate. As a giver, it should be expected. As a receiver, it should be commonly practiced. We are all powerful people, so we have the ability to determine whether we let what someone says to us that doesn't seem helpful affect us or not. We're to be humble in giving and bold, yet gracious, in receiving.

3. Put it on a shelf.

When I get a word that falls flat or feels confusing I put it on a shelf and say, "God, if this is you, take it down when You want me to explore it with You." I remember my husband and I got a word together that, frankly, I didn't like. I put it on a shelf and, lo and behold, about three years later, the wisdom from that word played out in our lives and I was so amazed! Without psychoanalyzing why I didn't like the word, I didn't completely dismiss it, I just put it on a shelf. When the time came, God reminded me of it and it became one of our anchor words in a tough season.

4. Weigh it against the New Testament standard.

Did it edify, encourage, and/or comfort you? If not, don't fear!!! A person's words are not more powerful than God Himself! If you're really upset, talk with God about it. Talk with Him about how it made you feel and ask Him for His thoughts about you. Additionally, talk with healthy community who can give you wise counsel and help you process it safely.

5. Give feedback.

If you have a relationship with the person, let them know how the word you got from them made you feel. A lady at church gave me a word once and I told her, "Thank you for sharing. The beginning of the word was awesome, but the end of the word was not accurate." I did it in love, but I didn't want her to leave not knowing her word was off. I may have been the only person to give her honest feedback that day. Giving feedback, in love, helps people grow. If the person you give feedback to is not open to input, it may give you an indication of where they're at. Pray for them.

6. Is It a Foretelling Word?

If it's truly a prophetic word with a foretelling (future) nature, it may not resonate with you at all. This is because it's not your present reality. If you get a word that you're an entrepreneur and you don't have a business bone in your body, it may just be that it's not your present reality. God loves to do miraculous things through unsuspecting people. This is an example of a word I'd put on a shelf. I'm convinced that God will resurrect it if it truly came from Him and He wants it to come to pass.

7. Gird your loins.

If we want to prophesy, we also need to be brave and be open to feedback. Just because we say evaluating should accompany the prophetic, won't always mean that we practice it. Fear can be a huge factor. Constructive feedback can be especially hard if we were raised in an environment where we couldn't be honest about our feelings or perfectionism was demanded. Conversely, it can also be a challenge for people who have no problem "speaking the truth." But in the Kingdom, everything we're to do is from a heart of love, which means it's okay if you make mistakes and it's okay if I make mistakes because we love and value one another. Might I suggest giving words to friends you know and trust and asking for feedback from them first? This will help ease you into the process of getting constructive feedback.

The Prophetic Is More Than Just Giving a Word

I want to encourage you not to compartmentalize or rigidly define your spiritual gifts. As I mentioned in chapter one, the gifts of the Spirit are often interrelated. For instance, the prophetic is more than just giving someone a word.

There is a whole world of prophetic out there that the Lord invites us into. Everything He shows us is an invitation to get close to Him and know Him more. The very nature of things in the Spirit is that they are out in front, ahead, or outside of time. God does not live in our time. He is always outside. His word says He actually sits enthroned above the circle of the earth and stretches the heavens out like a canopy (Isaiah 40:22).

Often God will show us things in the Spirit because He wants us to partner with Him in releasing His plans and purposes in the earth. As we carry on about our day God will speak to us, sometimes in a whisper, of things He'd like us to do with Him. The very nature of His invitation is prophetic, in that it's foretelling in nature. It requires a keen awareness of moving in the Spirit. Acts 17:28 says, "For in him we live and move and have our being."

One night I was going to speak at a prophetic home group. On the way, as I was thinking about my message on Spirit journeys, I heard God tell me very subtly to share my testimony. It was a still, small voice. I had absolutely no intention of sharing my testimony that night because I wanted to share on something mysterious and mystical! But I knew it was the Lord and I obeyed. As I began to give my testimony, the room was full of life and people were sitting on the edge of their seats. It was like you could hear a pin drop.

As I began to transition to what I *really* wanted to talk about that night, it was as if everyone fell asleep. It was like God sucked His breath out of the room. I said to the students, "Did you guys feel that? Did you sense a shift?" As I went around the room, I asked them what they were experiencing. A few people said it was like they got sleepy or distracted. One guy said he felt God's glory so I said, "Great! Stay there." I told them we were getting a live lesson in the prophetic. I went back to what God *was* breathing on and a guy raised his hand from behind the couch. I hadn't even seen him that night until that moment. I called on him and he said that he was going to commit suicide that day, but told God that if He would give him a message of hope he wouldn't kill himself. He said that everything I shared in my testimony is what he'd experienced in life. We invited him to the middle of the room and powerfully prayed for him. The night ended in a dance party as we all saw God orchestrate the evening around saving one of his precious children!

This was such a great learning experience for me in hearing and obeying God's voice. Often, we can have plans but aren't always open to those plans being interrupted. The Lord prophetically prepared me for what He wanted to release that night so He could save the life of this loved son of His. God's prophetic preparation positioned my heart and the gift of discernment helped me know how He was (and wasn't) moving. The nature of this prophetic discourse wasn't to give a prophetic word, per se, it was to prophetically show me how He wanted to move in that meeting.

Prophetic Asking

What have you been asking God for recently? Look back through your journals or letters to God. Your asking is often a prophetic picture of what's next for you! It says in Ecclesiastes 3:11 that He's placed eternity in our hearts. Our spirits know things that our minds can't comprehend. This knowing will sometimes manifest itself in the questions you ask God.

I remember one particular season I was continually asking God for wisdom in my prayer and journaling times. I wasn't sure *why* I was asking for wisdom other than when I would meet with Him, I would feel very *impressed* to continue to ask for it. I was drawn to Scriptures on wisdom, I had encounters with Him where He was depositing wisdom in me. For instance, once in a perceiving time, there was a large scroll full of wisdom and I sensed God feed it to me. It was delicious! It tasted like honey and I knew a spiritual impartation was happening. Finally, this season culminated in a dream. One night I dreamt and saw a big sign, like a billboard. On the sign were numbers and three blanks. It read, "404 _____ _____ _____." Being that I came from the technology industry when I worked in the business world, I immediately knew the blanks to mean "Page Not Found." Remember, God loves to speak our language. This message on the internet is commonly known as a "404 error." Knowing that I love a good challenge, God posed a riddle to me in a dream. I thought to myself, "Well, if it means 'Page Not Found,' I'm gonna find that page!" I went to my Bible and, lo and behold, on page 404 Solomon asks God for wisdom (1 Kings 3)!

In the season that followed, I lead a number of trips in which I needed to draw from the wisdom that He taught me in the previous season. Many challenges arise as we lead people and Godly wisdom is definitely needed in ensuring we lead with His heart. Although I wasn't sure why I was asking for wisdom at the time, my asking proved to be prophetic in nature as God was inviting me to get equipped for the season ahead.

Corporate Prophetic

If you find yourself ministering in a corporate environment, the Lord will often show you things prophetically that He wants you to release over the congregation. As He shows us what He wants to do in the environment, we can ask Him how He wants us to partner with Him. Sometimes it's releasing a prophetic word to the group through declaration, other times it's an invitation for prophetic intercession.

Prophetic Intercession

The Lord also speaks to us prophetically so we can partner with Him to bind and loose (see the chapter entitled, "The Honor of a King and Priest"). This type of intercession can be for individuals, corporate bodies, geographical regions, and nations.

With prophetic intercession, we don't simply launch into prayer. Either He will show us things or we ask Him what's on His heart. Then we partner with Him to release what He shows us by declaration. Job 22:28 says, "You will also declare a thing, and it will be established for you." (NKJV) The Holy Spirit knows what's needed in any situation and often God doesn't need our many words.

For several years, as a school, we would meet before service at church and ask God what He wanted to do that night. As we'd ask and wait, He would show us pictures, give us impressions, Scripture verses, or lyrics to a worship song. Rather than just blindly pray, we would position our hearts to partner with God, through declaration, in what He wanted to release during the services. The testimonies were amazing as God would do in the services the very things He had shown us! We had the honor of seeing what we declared come to pass and our faith skyrocketed.

To Delight Your Heart

One time during a worship service I was praying for my sister, her husband, and two children. In my prayer I said, "and the new little one." I was shocked and amazed at what came out of my mouth, but knew immediately they were expecting another baby. I almost called her but I decided to ponder it in my heart until and unless it was confirmed. I got a text soon after that she was pregnant! Now, this was a word of knowledge in that God told me information about them that I couldn't have known on my own, but it was also prophetic in nature in that it was a future event.

God shared His heart with me, I declared it, and thanked Him for what He showed me. I knew this was God letting me in more to His world. I discovered that day that God will show us things in advance just to delight our hearts.

The Word

The Bible *is* prophetic because it's the inspired Word of God. It becomes personally prophetic when the Holy Spirit highlights or causes something to jump off the page just for you. This is known as the *rhema* word.[60] Matthew 4:4 says, "It is written, 'Man shall not live by bread alone, but by every word that proceeds from the mouth of God.'" (NKJV) "Word" here is translated from *rhema* in the Greek and it means a word that has been *"uttered by the living voice"* of God. This type of "prophetic word" requires no judging or weighing because it comes straight from God's heart to you. As you're reading the Word and a particular Scripture is emphasized to you by the Lord, it's Him saying, "This is what I'm about to do in your life," or "This is the hope you need for the circumstances you're facing." We have a tendency to hold the prophetic words of man in a higher place than the Scriptures but this is error and, quite frankly, a sad substitute for the counsel, guidance, and words of hope for an amazing future from the Creator of the universe!

Food for Thought

There are some things that I'd like to present for your consideration as you're developing your prophetic gift.

- Sometimes you can know that the Lord wants you to share a prophetic word with someone but won't tell you till you get there. He wants you to step out in faith (risk) and trust Him. It's exhilarating when we do!

- If I feel fear before I give a prophetic word, it's often because that's the very thing the Lord wants to say to the person, but the enemy is contesting it. Push through the fear and deliver the word. You'll be amazed at how "right on" and timely the word will be.

- I rarely give a correctional or directional prophetic word. I believe these words are best given by people with whom we're in community. These types of words give input on life changes and life direction. That's kind of scary when you think about it! I personally don't want people changing the course of their lives based on a word I've given them. Additionally, when we're in relationship with people that we do give correctional or directional words to, purpose to give those people permission to provide constructive feedback. It's good for them to know that they will have a healthy environment in which to process the word. When I do strongly sense a correctional or directional word for a friend, I will frame it up with a very humble, "For your consideration…" or "Can I submit to you…?"

  If we have a deep need to tell someone that they should be living their life differently, we begin to operate in the realm of the flesh through assumption and judgment. Giving directional words also gives us a false sense of power at times. This is how the prophetic moves into manipulation and control. As you can see, this is about internal motivation, not inspiration from the Lord.

Ultimately, we want people to get their direction from Jesus, with the input of wise counsel through community. We don't want people anchoring themselves to us. When the storms of life get crazy we want them anchored to Jesus, the Hope and Author of their story.

An example of a directional word gone bad happened many years ago. A friend of ours received a word from an itinerant minister in a public setting. The speaker had our friend stand up in front of the whole congregation and said they would meet their spouse within the next 12 months. Twelve months passed, two years passed, four years passed, still no spouse. This was devastating for our friend. Wondering if they missed the voice of God, potentially worrying about sin in their life or pondering if they should fast more, desperate to find their mate, this word created a lot of confusion and heartache for many years. The itinerant minister, on the other hand, got to go home and move on with life. There was no opportunity for accountability this errant word created in the life of our precious friend.

- Don't be dogmatic! God often releases prophetic words through us to give people hope to endure life's storms. He knows we need a glimpse of our future to stay the course. Jesus endured the cross because of the promise He could see. When we can see the future, we can endure the present, too. Is Jesus the true and only Hope we're to anchor ourselves to? Yes, of course. But we can't get dogmatic about what that means and completely shut down the prophetic. God chooses to use people as His mouthpiece. Our dogma can sometimes rob people of an encounter with God.

- In all reality, I don't think we can prophesy without discernment being operational. The two work together beautifully. We discern what God's saying and we declare it. So fun!

- Be aware of distracting behaviors. The whole point of the prophetic is to communicate a word to someone for the Lord. We're merely the vessel He's speaking through. So, we don't want to get in the way. Revealing clothing or talking too quietly, for instance, can be distracting and make it difficult for the hearer to receive.

- Does it feel better to receive an encouraging word or a disparaging word? It's not a trick question. No one likes to receive a bad word. Our job is to give a word that encourages. A good way to discern what you're sensing in the process of giving a prophetic word is to determine which of these two categories it falls in. If what you're getting for someone is negative it might be your own flesh, it might be the enemy, or it may even be what you're picking up from that particular person (yes, that's possible). It's easy to see the issues in someone's life and the enemy likes to be demonstrative. The Holy Spirit, on the other hand, is usually very subtle.

We have to look past the outward appearance and ask God to show us what He sees! In 1 Samuel 16, Samuel went to anoint the king in Jesse's house and he, erroneously, looked for the manliest man. He saw one of Jesse's strapping sons and said, "Certainly the Lord's anointed one is here before Him." But the Lord told him, no; "Man does not see what the Lord sees, for man sees what is visible but the Lord sees the heart." Press in to the Holy

Spirit for what God is saying about the person you're ministering to. Only He knows what's in their heart and what He's knitted in them. The gifts He may tell you to call forth might seem like the biggest stretch imaginable!

- Sometimes I think, "Am I just making this up?" I often find those are the most right-on words.

- Purity is a key to the prophetic. Matthew 5:7 says the pure in heart will see God. If we want to see what God's doing, we have to keep our hearts pure from the things that would taint us. Yes, like pornography, but also things like gossip, offense, and pride. In Acts 21, we see that Philip the evangelist had four virgin daughters who prophesied. I believe this verse further suggests that purity is tied to the prophetic. Does this mean we all have to be celibate? No. It's a principle that we can take from this verse. Keep your channel clear and your heart pure. Often the word of the Lord is filtered through our hearts and minds and the purer they are, the purer the word can be.

Reflection

1. What is the only requirement to prophesying? _____

2. 1 Corinthians 14:1 tells us to do three things. What are they? _____

   _____

3. What is the one main difference between being a prophet and a believer who prophesies?

   _____

4. Why do you think it's so important to God's heart that we prophesy in love? _____

   _____

5. Why do you think it's important to God that we prophesy at all? _____

   _____

6. If we're giving a New Testament prophetic word, what three things will the person receiving feel (the by-products)?

   _____

7. There are three components/parts to a prophetic word. What are they and who is responsible for each?

   _____

   _____

8. Give an example of a time when you used a spiritual gift from a heart of love. _____

   _____

   _____

9. Why is it important to develop your own dictionary with the Lord? _____

   _____

Activation

We're going to do a few activations in this section to help you get comfortable with taking risk in the prophetic.

Activation #1

It's important that you follow the steps of this activation for the Holy Spirit to blow your mind!

- Step #1 - Get alone with the Lord and ask Him for a prophetic word for someone (don't ask who and don't pick someone). Just ask for a prophetic word.
- Step #2 - Type that word into your phone or computer (you can also write it on paper if you don't like technology).
- Step #3 - Go to Facebook, Instagram, etc. or your email contacts (a good old fashioned address book will do, too) and ask Holy Spirit who the word is for.
- Step #4 - Send it to them privately and watch how awesome God is!

Activation #2

When you're out running errands, ask the Holy Spirit to highlight someone to you and give you a prophetic word for them. Approach the person and tell them that God pointed them out to you. Tell them you believe He has a word for them and ask if you can share it. Now, sometimes we can get a skeptical or grumpy person. All the more reason to *ask* if we can share. Sure, they may say no. But I have had very few people actually tell me "no." Most of the time if we're humble and kind, they will be open to hearing all the good things God has to say about them! Be brave!

Activation #3

Tell a close family member or friend that you have a homework assignment. Ask if you can give them a prophetic word in person or over the phone and let them know you are specifically looking for constructive feedback: Did the word encourage or comfort them? Did they feel the love of God in the word? Could you have worded something differently? Take this feedback and continue to develop your prophetic gift.

Activation #4

Continue to broaden your spiritual understanding and develop your dictionary by asking the Holy Spirit to give you definitions for the symbols on the next page.

Birds	A hammer
The color yellow	A car
An RV/bus	Springtime
A wall	Oil
A well	An egg

Visions

"...I will move on to visions and revelations of the Lord."
2 Corinthians 12:1b

Who wants to go places in the Spirit? I do! I do! Pick me!!! As you can tell, I love visions, Spirit journeys, and supernatural experiences with the Lord. Spending time in intimacy with Him and the awe and wonder of revealed mysteries is so incredible. Having Him show me things that bends my brain but excites my spirit, never gets old.

The more we spend time with God, the more we get to know Him and His world. We often sing songs about seeing Him one day when we get to heaven, but I believe that we can have incredible experiences here on this side of the veil. I'm convinced that when I go to heaven and meet Jesus, I won't be completely shocked or surprised by what I see because I've cultivated a heavenly, spiritual reality with Him here while I'm on the earth. Certainly, there will be countless new things to explore because we will never get to the end of discovering Him!

Visions are another language in which God communicates with us. These visions can go beyond one-dimensional pictures to interactive encounters with God. The more we cultivate hunger, expectation, and child-like belief, the more we can grow in dynamic, technicolor visions that can even play out in different scenes or over a period of time.

Keys to Cultivating and Increasing Visions in Our Lives

1. Create an expectation and hunger for spiritual experiences with the Lord.

In order to expand your spiritual experiences, you have to believe that they're available. As you will see in this chapter, there is a ton of Biblical precedent for visions. Be available, full of faith, and expectant. Take "can't" and "shouldn't" out of your vocabulary.

2. Tell your mind (logic) to rest.

Our minds can be opposed to the things of the Spirit. Although the Bible tells us that we are a new creation and we have the mind of Christ, our flesh man cannot comprehend the things of the Spirit. It's helpful to be aware of this and allow your mind to rest. A good way to know if logic is getting in the way is if objections start popping up left and right.

3. Give your spirit permission to receive from the Lord.

I bless my spirit to lead me and be lead of the Holy Spirit. This reinforces the message I send my mind to rest.

4. Get in a comfortable, conducive place to receive.

We have a little room under our staircase that I've converted into my prayer closet. This is where I spend a lot of time with God. It's quiet, away from the demands of the house, and I can focus on Him without distraction.

5. The only guide we have is the Holy Spirit.

Like I mentioned in an earlier chapter, I don't communicate with angels or other spiritual beings. Also, I don't force myself into spiritual experiences. I always pray and tell the Lord I'm available. Often, I will ask Him where He wants to take me. Sometimes He and I don't go on a journey, other times we do. But I don't decide that. I let Him lead me and I follow. The only add-on to this is that any place He takes me is mine to access at any time. However, as I recall a place that I've visited frequently, like my garden in heaven, and He doesn't seem to be there, I turn my attention to Him and sense where He *is* working.

Why Visions?

We have visions because God wants to talk with us. He wants to invite us more into His world and His affairs here on the earth. Processing what we see in visions happens with our spirit man, often through our renewed mind and our five senses, as we discovered in the chapter on discernment. Being intentional about allowing our logic to take a back seat is imperative as we position ourselves to receive from the Lord.

"...but I will move on to visions and revelations of the Lord. I know a man in Christ who was caught up into the third heaven 14 years ago. Whether he was in the body or out of the body, I don't know, God knows. I know that this man—whether in the body or out of the body I don't know, God knows—was caught up into paradise. He heard inexpressible words, which a man is not allowed to speak."

2 Corinthians 12:1b - 4

As we see in this passage by Paul, sometimes visions are hard to explain. This is why getting into a theological argument with someone about whether or not what you experience is valid can be pointless. How do we accurately put language to an experience that is super-natural? Paul wasn't even sure if he was in the body or out of the body (Paul was the man he was referring to, by the way. Most likely to protect himself from pride and boasting in the flesh, he de-personalized the experience).

I remember years ago when my husband and I were first married, we were going through a rough patch, as all married couples do. I was at a church service and went up for prayer at the end of the evening. The pastor's wife approached me and said, "God wants to meet you in your garden." I had no idea what that meant, but it "felt" right. Fast-forward about eight years. I was going through a season where God was pulling fear out of my life by the root. It was one of the hardest seasons of my life. One day, I was pacing back and forth, full of anxiety, in our room and my husband said, "I don't know how to help you." I knew that I had to get alone with God. I went into our closet and told God that I wasn't leaving until the pain lifted. As I was there, crying out for help, I pictured being in a garden with Jesus. I wrapped my hands around His feet and let my tears fall on them as I cried and cried. Finally, a peace came that I couldn't have conjured up. The anxiety broke and I felt restful. As the years went on, I began to have many encounters with Jesus in a garden. The garden, in fact, began to expand. There were tall hedges, green grass, and a cool stone bench where we would meet.

One day, as I was researching the above passage from 2 Corinthians 12, I was amazed at my discovery. The word "paradise" that Paul uses there is translated *garden* from the Greek![61] All those years I was having a real, transcendent experience with Jesus in my very own paradise!

Delving into the Word and relying on the Holy Spirit is key to understanding what we see and experience in these types of Spirit adventures. There is a ton of Biblical precedent for visions and it can serve to help us define our own experiences and understand certain principles related to the visions God gives us.

As we build our dictionary with Him, we can more quickly interpret what He's showing us. Although, the beauty of a journey with Jesus is that He often invites us into mysteries we get to ponder for a long time, with little understanding at first, but a great sense of awe.

On one occasion as I was spending time with the Lord, I was caught up in a vision and all of a sudden I was in a wormhole, going lightning speed in the Spirit. Immediately, I was hovering over a tiny tropical island. As quickly as I got to the island, I was back in the wormhole and then, immediately, was hovering over a European-type city. The vision ended. To this day, I have no idea which island or city it was or even why I had that vision. I'm sure one day I will know, but for now, it remains a mystery. A very exciting mystery!

It is important to know that we can grow in our experiences of visions and Spirit journeys. As with all spiritual things, stewardship and availability lead to increase. As we cherish and nurture the things God shows us we, essentially, tell Him we value Him. The more we value Him, the more He invites us in.

Lastly, I won't limit the Holy Spirit's ability to show me things or take me places by man's interpretation of the Word. My go-to is the Word itself, not commentaries, common teachings, or other people's experiences (or lack thereof). If it's in the Word, it's mine by legal access through Jesus.

Biblical Definitions

Let's look at some Hebrew and Greek words and definitions from Strong's Concordance for visions and other spiritual experiences.

Hebrew

1. *Makhazeh* – A vision in the ecstatic state.[62]

An ecstatic state can be a trance-like condition where all natural surroundings are tuned out. The root of this Hebrew word means "to see, perceive, look, prophesy" or "to see as a seer in the ecstatic state."

2. *Mar'ah* – A vision, mode of revelation.[63]

The root word here means "sight, appearance, vision (supernatural), power of seeing." The primitive root means "to see, perceive, watch."

3. *Chazown* – A vision in the ecstatic state, in the night, oracle, prophecy.[64]

The root of this word means "to see, perceive, look, prophesy."

Greek

1. *Ekstasis* – This definition is amazing. It reads, "A throwing of the mind out of its normal state, alienation of mind, whether such as make a lunatic or that of a man who by some sudden emotion is transported as it were out of himself, so that in this rapt condition, although he is awake, his mind is drawn off from all surrounding objects and wholly fixed on things divine that he sees nothing but the forms and images lying within, and thinks that he perceives with his bodily eyes and ears realities shown him by God."[65]

This also is a trance-like state. In looking more closely at the above definition, it says, "whether such as make a lunatic or that of a man who by some sudden emotion is transported as it were out of himself." It's interesting to note that Joan of Arc was accused of being a lunatic for her professed ecstatic experiences.

2. *Optasia* – A sight, vision.[66]

This is further defined as "…an appearance presented to one whether asleep or awake." We see here that visions can be similar to dreams at night. The root means "to look at, behold."

3. *Apokalypsis* – Laying bare, a disclosure of truth.[67]

Don't even get me started on the apocalypse! The real apocalypse is when the sons and daughters of God are revealed to the earth and the Kingdom of heaven continually transforms this world through Christ in us, the hope of glory. Yet, I digress... This word *apokalypsis* further means "used of events by which things or states or persons hitherto withdrawn from view are made visible." It's root means "to make known." It's simply a revelation or revealing of what's been hidden.

Biblical Precedent for Visions

We are going to take a walk through the Bible to look at some of the visions and ecstatic experiences that different people had with God. This is not an exhaustive, all-inclusive look but it's a good snapshot that I hope inspires you to hunger for more!

1. Abram (later Abraham)

"After these events, the word of the Lord came to Abram in a vision: 'Do not be afraid, Abram. I am your shield; your reward will be very great.'" – Genesis 15:1

God appeared to Abram. He came to him in a *machazeh*, an ecstatic state. In this passage, He promised Abram a son. God then took him outside and said, "Look up at the sky and count all the stars – if indeed you can count them...so shall your offspring be (Genesis 15:5)." In fact, in this encounter with God, Abram was promised countless heirs. As a result of this ecstatic experience and given promise, Abram believed God and it was credited to him as righteousness (see Hebrews 11). God, too, gives us prophetic promises in visions.

2. Jacob (also Israel)

"That night God spoke to Israel in a vision: 'Jacob, Jacob!' He said. And Jacob replied, 'Here I am.'" – Genesis 46:2

God spoke to Jacob in a *mar'ah* in the night. Israel was afraid to go to Egypt because he wasn't sure if his most loved son, Joseph, was really alive. In this encounter, God ensured Jacob it was his son, Joseph. Sometimes it's hard to differentiate dreams at night from actual encounters with the Lord. The take-away from these encounters is that they are Spirit to spirit. And for Israel, there was no denying God had spoken to him to give him direction and encouragement.

3. Moses

"Listen to what I say: If there is a prophet among you from the Lord, I make Myself known to him in a vision; I speak with him in a dream. Not so with My servant Moses; he is faithful in all My household. I speak with him directly, openly, and not in riddles; he sees the form of the Lord." – Numbers 12:6-8

There's so much that I love about these few verses and the greater context of the passage. Miriam and Aaron are grumbling about Moses and the Lord hears it. The Bible says, "Moses was a very humble man, more so than any man on the face of the earth." God commanded all three of them to come out of the tent of meeting so He could address the jealousy and complaining of Moses' siblings. I am moved to tears to know that not only does God defend us, but that humility is tied to seeing Him. And by seeing Him, I don't just mean visions and dreams, but actually *seeing* God. This passage indicates that not only are visions, dreams, and spiritual experiences available, but so is having direct encounters with God. Again, if it's in the Word, there's precedent for us. If He spoke with Moses directly, I want to speak with Him directly, too!

4. Ezekiel

"In the thirtieth year, in the fourth month, on the fifth day of the month, while I was among the exiles by the Chebar Canal, the heavens opened and I saw visions of God." - Ezekiel 1:1

Why, yes. Yes, I do want to have a *mar'ah* where the heavens open and I see visions of God. The book of Ezekiel is an incredible book full of descriptive details, colors, and imagery. Ezekiel was a priest who had extraordinary visions and prophesied to nations on behalf of God. God wants to give us visions so we can prophesy on His behalf, as well.

5. Daniel

"Daniel also understood visions and dreams of every kind." Daniel 1:17

Daniel is one of my favorite people in the Bible. He came from upper class Israelites, was very intelligent, wise, and handsome, yet he was very humble and honoring. How many times do we rely solely on our talents and abilities and leave little room for Kingdom principles and call? Daniel demonstrated throughout the course of his life and captivity (which spanned multiple kings) that he was submitted and dedicated to the one and only true God. He was living in Babylon but fully committed to the Kingdom of Heaven. He even took on a Babylonian name! But never wavered in His Kingdom identity. Daniel had a remarkable life of visions, supernatural encounters, and dreams. I would suggest it was due, in part, to the way he stewarded his life. True, we don't do anything to qualify ourselves, but there are things we can do to position ourselves for increase.

6. Peter

"The next day, as they were traveling and nearing the city, Peter went up to pray on the housetop about noon. Then he became hungry and wanted to eat, but while they were preparing something, he went into a visionary state. He saw heaven opened and an object that resembled a large sheet coming down, being lowered by its four corners to the earth. In it were all the four-footed animals and reptiles of the earth, and the birds of the sky. Then a voice said to him, "Get up, Peter; kill and eat!" – Acts 10:9-13

Peter fell into a trance. Let's revisit the definition for this Greek word *ekstasis:* "A throwing of the mind out of its normal state, alienation of mind, whether such as makes a lunatic or that of a man who by some sudden emotion is transported as it were out of himself, so that in this rapt condition, although he is awake, his mind is drawn off from all surrounding objects and wholly fixed on things divine that he sees nothing but the forms and images lying within, and thinks that he perceives with his bodily eyes and ears realities shown him by God."

Isn't that amazing!? When God really wants to get our attention, He knows how to do it! In this definition, we see that the person receiving the vision actually believes that they are perceiving with their natural eyes and ears. Peter was transfixed on the vision God gave Him because God needed Peter's undivided attention. His message: Minister to the Gentiles! The vision was repeated three times for emphasis and the Holy Spirit aided Peter in the interpretation. When Peter got to Cornelius' house he knew what God was saying: call no man was impure or unclean what Jesus has made clean. Salvation came to the Gentiles through a vision!

7. Paul

"...but I will move on to visions and revelations of the Lord. I know a man in Christ who was caught up into the third heaven 14 years ago. Whether he was in the body or out of the body, I don't know, God knows. I know that this man—whether in the body or out of the body I don't know, God

knows— was caught up into paradise. He heard inexpressible words, which a man is not allowed to speak." - 2 Corinthians 12:1b-4

Paul is another one of my favorite people in the Bible. He was called as a sent one, an apostle, of God to extend the Kingdom on earth, to show people what heaven was like, and to equip them for Kingdom life. Paul's first encounter with Jesus on the road to Damascus was quite supernatural. And, from this passage in 2 Corinthians, we know these types of experiences were the standard for Paul. He had visions and revelations from God, some of which he was not permitted to share. That's some real trust-building! The two words visions and revelations, are *optasia* and *apokalysis*, respectively. Remember, the first word, *optasia*, means "a sight, vision, an appearance presented to one whether asleep or awake." The second word, *apokalypsis*, means "laying bare, a disclosure of truth." God revealed truths to Paul to aid him in his call and gave him visions of paradise, promises to, no doubt, help him through many trials. When we get glimpses of eternity through visions and revelation, it makes our momentary, light afflictions of this world bearable and helps keep persecutions in perspective.

8. John the Revelator

"After this I looked, and there in heaven was an open door. The first voice that I had heard speaking to me like a trumpet said, "Come up here, and I will show you what must take place after this." Immediately I was in the Spirit, and a throne was set there in heaven. One was seated on the throne, and the One seated looked like jasper and carnelian stone. A rainbow that looked like an emerald surrounded the throne. Around that throne were 24 thrones, and on the thrones sat 24 elders dressed in white clothes, with gold crowns on their heads. Flashes of lightning and rumblings of thunder came from the throne. Seven fiery torches were burning before the throne, which are the seven spirits of God. Something like a sea of glass, similar to crystal, was also before the throne. Four living creatures covered with eyes in front and in back were in the middle and around the throne. The first living creature was like a lion; the second living creature was like a calf; the third living creature had a face like a man; and the fourth living creature was like a flying eagle. Each of the four living creatures had six wings; they were covered with eyes around and inside. Day and night they never stop, saying:

Holy, holy, holy,
Lord God, the Almighty,
who was, who is, and who is coming." – Revelation 4:1-8

You know you have some crazy encounters with God when your last name is "the Revelator." Just kidding. That's not really his last name but it's sometimes how he is referred to as the writer of the book of Revelation. Chapter one, verse one indicates that this revelation, which is the word *apokalypsis,* is of Jesus Christ. The writer, John, is commonly believed to be the apostle John. He was very close to Jesus. In the Gospel of John, he even refers to himself as the "disciple whom Jesus loved."[68] We see from this close relationship that the fruit of intimacy is revelation. With that being said, we have some great take-aways from the above passage in the book of Revelation. While I could write an entire section on Revelation chapter four alone, let's take a peek at just a few observations: 1) John's vision was incredibly detailed and vivid, employing the senses of sight and hearing (much like Ezekiel's visions, which also refer to the four living creatures), 2) John was "in the Spirit" during the vision. Supernatural experiences are accessed by the Spirit. 3) Heaven is not boring! There is a lot of activity going on here. 4) Jesus is breathtakingly beautiful! 5) The angels only have one song, "Holy, holy, holy."

Have you ever wondered how the throne Jesus sits on is a rainbow displayed in an emerald tone? I have. I can't imagine the beauty of it. John was using the best language he had to describe a heavenly reality. When we have visions, it will often be hard to describe some of what we see because it requires that we put language to things that are not of this world.

More on Visions

When we positon ourselves to receive from God, we can increase in visions and supernatural encounters. The Lord gives us visions because He is inviting us into deeper relationship with Him. God is not limited to the "why's" we have, but He does long for us to become more aware of the purpose of visions so we can be more intentional about yet another aspect of our relationship with Him.

1. Visions can be directional in nature.

When we were called to leave Redding, CA, God spoke to us in so many ways that Phoenix, AZ was to be our next destination. I remember during the transition, before we had decided on Phoenix, I was on the couch one morning and went into a vivid vision. I was interrupted a couple times by the phone and my husband heading out to work, but knowing there is no time and space in the Spirit, I purposed to go right back into the vision. When I reconnected, I was with God in outer space. It was amazing up there! There were stars all around and a beautiful black blanket covering the sky. He was standing next to me as a Father Time type figure (I now refer to Him from this vision as the Father of Time in certain situations). As we were up there together, He cast a few images onto the backdrop of black, sprinkled with little lights. Among other things, He showed me a symbol of a star with rays coming off it and luggage with the numbers "3+4." After the vision, I researched Arizona only to find out that the state flag is exactly as He showed me in the vision, a star with rays coming out! Shortly thereafter, we knew we were moving and settled on July (the seventh month of the year. 3+4=7). This vision solidified our direction and gave me peace and confidence about our next steps.

2. Visions open up our spirits.

Ecclesiastes 3:11 says that He's placed eternity in our hearts. Visions prepare our spirits for what God wants to do in our lives by drawing from that place of eternity within us.

3. Visions can prepare us for our call.

If we are careful about stewarding what He shows us, we find that God is always ahead of and outside of time. He knows what we need before we even ask! Steward what He shows you by recording or journaling your journey. He will always equip you for what He calls you to and often this can happen in visions.

4. Visions build our faith.

It is so faith-building to have a detailed vision confirmed in Scripture or have it play out in the natural. I still get amazed like a little kid at what the Holy Spirit reveals to me in visions that I discover are backed up by the Word or something that transpires in life shortly after He shows me. My faith goes to new levels.

5. Visions can facilitate going places in the Spirit with the Lord.

I call these "Spirit journeys." Many times, I'm with the Lord and He'll take me places around the world. I think the place I've visited the most is India. Jesus loves India so much! One time I started praying in tongues and immediately I was in a Spirit journey up over the country. I looked out over India and it was dark outside. Then I saw tiny lights popping up all over the country. Worship rose up to the Lord like incense from little groups all over the land. I thanked the Lord for the small groups of people who loved Him in India and were worshipping Him. I blessed the country to have increased encounters with His love and that more people would come to know Him. This vision inspired an acknowledgment of what was on His heart through intercession (a priestly function we'll explore more in the chapter on intercession) and declaration.

6. Visions can be similar to dreams.

Like dreams, visions are usually symbolic in nature and may require some interpretation. It's important to continue to build your dictionary with the Lord. Your personal language and history with Him will help you interpret what He's saying, as will your gift of discernment. Like dreams, visions may have an immediate application or play out over time. Unlike dreams, however, I would suggest that visions don't require as much sorting through the metaphor, symbolism, and source (because the Spirit initiates and we discern His peace and love as we're experiencing a vision). Dreams are often generated from our soul/mind and can be the internal processing of our lives (we will cover in the chapter on dreams).

7. Visions are referred to in different ways.

We can also call visions seeing in the Spirit, spiritual experiences, downloads, etc. Again, whether closed or open, all are valid.

8. Visions can be positive or negative.

I don't often have negative spiritual experiences. However, I have had some of these encounters. While I did not initiate them, God taught me *so much* through them. If God allows you to have a negative vision or experience, there is always a spiritual principle or lesson that He wants to teach you. He will always give you a solution or heavenly answer to partner with Him in applying. For instance, perhaps God wants to show us an open door of access that we've allowed to the enemy or He wants to teach us something about our authority in Jesus. One demonic encounter that I had, although scary, was incredible. God taught me that there are certain situations that will *only* shift if we pray in tongues. The enemy can mimic our Christian songs, he even knows Scripture (see Matthew 4), but he can't interpret the language of heaven.

10. Tongues are a big key.

Speaking in tongues during your prayer time can be a big component in receiving visions. It acts as a conduit between your spirit and the Holy Spirit.

Food for Thought

- I would encourage you to de-compartmentalize visions. Sometimes, in our journey of defining spiritual things, we put them in neat little boxes and limit ourselves and the Lord! Whether it be an open vision, a closed vision in your mind's eye, a daydream, lucid dreaming, or an encounter at night, I would encourage you to look at them all as spiritual experiences. Don't immediately go down the checklist of which ones you do and don't have or can or can't have. Let the Lord know you're open to them all!

- Sometimes we have experiences that are difficult to explain. During worship one time, I saw myself spinning around the Godhead praising and worshipping Them. As I was spinning around Them, I began to prophesy to Them. In the vision, I didn't know what I was saying, I just knew that I was prophesying. Afterwards, I was like, "whaaaaaaat?" How can I *prophesy* to the Lord? That didn't seem, you know, legal. But when you spend a lot of time with Him, He will invite you into a place of counsel. It may sound crazy, but Abraham was bold enough to ask that the residents of Sodom be spared if God could find just 10 righteous people in the city!

- Many of the gifts of the Spirit are interrelated to visions: discernment, prophecy, word of knowledge, word of wisdom, etc. Miracles, signs, and wonders can be birthed out of visions with the Lord! He can impart a grace for what He wants to accomplish through you during these remarkable times of intimacy.

- There are always new levels!!! All it takes is your availability, asking, and belief!

Reflection

1. Why are visions available for us today? _____

_____

2. How are our five senses and mind utilized during a vision? _____

_____

3. How can you be available, full of faith, and expectant to experience visions? _____

_____

4. Reflect on times where you think God was talking to you through a vision. Write it down.

_____

_____

5. Choose one of the Biblical people in this chapter, or a different one of your choice, and read more about his/her experiences with God.

Activation

Activation #1

Spend some time with the Lord. Prepare yourself with worship music and a distraction-free environment. Ask the Lord where He would like to take you or what He would like to show you. Pray in tongues. Write down your experience. If He takes you somewhere, where is it? Ask Him about it. If He shows you pictures, ask Him what they mean. Anything the Lord shows you is always yours! No one can take it away from you.

Side note: If you don't speak in tongues and would like to, guess what!? God wants you to, as well. I would invite you to pray this prayer: *"God, I believe that tongues are available to us as believers today. I want to speak in tongues and believe that by Your Holy Spirit I can. Activate this gift in me, by Your Spirit. I bless my mind to rest. In Jesus' Name, Amen."* Start speaking, even if it's just a few syllables. It may feel awkward but that's okay! It takes some practice. Practice in the shower, in the car, or wherever you feel comfortable.

Activation #2

Get alone with God and ask Him to show you your garden or some other place that He's prepared for you. Write down your experience and dialogue with Him on it.

Colors, Numbers, and Repetitions

"He reveals the deep and hidden things..."
Daniel 2:22

As you're learning in this manual, God speaks in many different ways. He does this because He loves talking with us, there's no end to His creativity, and He doesn't want us to become complacent in our walk with Him. God has a limitless toolbox of things that He can use to delight us in partnering with Him in extending the Kingdom in the earth. We can become increasingly *open* to His world, the ways of the Spirit, as we become increasingly *aware* of it.

Being available to Him and experiencing His Presence is as simple as giving your attention to Him. He is just a thought away. As we listen, we learn. Then, what He begins to show us, we can steward well to graduate, in a sense, to the next level of partnership.

In this chapter, we're going to talk about some of the other ways that He speaks to us. As we've mentioned in previous chapters, with the things of the Spirit it's good to pay attention to the things that get your attention. God is not limited in the way He speaks and often it will be in ways that are extraordinary and awe-inspiring.

Prophetic Colors

God is the ultimate Artist, Clothing Designer, Interior Decorator, and Creator. If we take off our "religious" lenses and simply look around at His world with wonder, we can see that He loves to create! And He does it very well.

The Bible is loaded with colors. Looking in the book of Exodus where God was giving the instructions for the tabernacle and priestly garments, you'll see that He is incredibly intentional about design. He was very specific when He shared with Moses about the colors, woods, metals and fabrics to be used. The level of detail is astounding.

"You are to make an embroidered breastpiece for making decisions. Make it with the same workmanship as the ephod; make it of gold, of blue, purple, and scarlet yarn, and of finely spun linen. It must be square and folded double, nine inches long and nine inches wide. Place a setting of gemstones on it, four rows of stones: The first row should be a row of carnelian, topaz, and emerald; the second row, a turquoise, a sapphire, and a diamond; the third row, a jacinth, an agate, and an amethyst; and the fourth row, a beryl, an onyx, and a jasper. They should be adorned with gold filigree in their settings. The 12 stones are to correspond to the names of Israel's sons. Each stone must be engraved like a seal, with one of the names of the 12 tribes.

"You are to make braided chains of pure gold cord work for the breastpiece. Fashion two gold rings for the breastpiece and attach them to its two corners. Then attach the two gold cords to the two gold rings at the corners of the breastpiece. Attach the other ends of the two cords to the two filigree settings, and in this way attach them to the ephod's shoulder pieces in the front. Make two other gold rings and put them at the two other corners of the breastpiece on the edge that is next to the inner border of the ephod. Make two more gold rings and attach them to the bottom of the ephod's two shoulder pieces on its front, close to its seam, and above the ephod's woven waistband. The craftsmen are to tie the breastpiece from its rings to the rings of the ephod with a cord of blue yarn, so that the breastpiece is above the ephod's waistband and does not come loose from the ephod. Whenever he enters the sanctuary, Aaron is to carry the names of Israel's sons over his heart on the breastpiece for decisions, as a continual reminder before the Lord. Place the

Urim and Thummim in the breastpiece for decisions, so that they will also be over Aaron's heart whenever he comes before the Lord. Aaron will continually carry the means of decisions for the Israelites over his heart before the Lord.

"You are to make the robe of the ephod entirely of blue yarn. There should be an opening at its top in the center of it. Around the opening, there should be a woven collar with an opening like that of body armor so that it does not tear. Make pomegranates of blue, purple, and scarlet yarn on its lower hem and all around it. Put gold bells between them all the way around, so that gold bells and pomegranates alternate around the lower hem of the robe. The robe must be worn by Aaron whenever he ministers, and its sound will be heard when he enters the sanctuary before the Lord and when he exits, so that he does not die."

Exodus 28:15 - 35

God gave Moses the instructions on what the place of worship was to look like and what the priests were to wear, in order to minister to God on behalf of the people. It's not because God was a control freak. If we take our fleshly or religious views out of the way, we see that God's color palette in Exodus is one of intentionality. If we read this passage with child-like wonder and heart of a learner, we can see that each color, each stone, each thread of yarn, must have had a purpose. God could have easily said, "Make a temple and wear some clothes. Oh, and make it nice." But He didn't do that. He instructed Moses with an incredible amount of detail. So, we can ask ourselves what the purpose of each color and symbol was. In fact, this is yet another language in which God is inviting us to learn about.

As we saw in the previous chapter on visions, the book of Revelation has some jaw-dropping colors, as well. God's throne, as described in Revelation chapter four, is surrounded in a rainbow that looks like an emerald! Have you ever thought about that verse? How is that even possible? A rainbow in a green tone. Hmm. John the Revelator probably used the best language he had to describe the beauties of heaven.

The Lord loves to speak to *us* through colors. Understanding this language is similar to the other languages of the Spirit. As with the other metaphors and images, it's often about understanding the symbolism. This understanding comes through learning the Bible, applying the rule of first mention, reading other resources, building your own dictionary with the Lord, and using your discerner.

I often experience the Lord in colors. When I'm in my perceiving times with Him, He shows me things prophetically in colors. As I've grown in relationship with Him, I usually instinctively know what the colors mean but this has taken some time to develop.

I had an experience once in a worship time where the Holy Spirit was pouring over me like an amber substance. I had such a warm, peaceful feeling as He poured over me in love. As I began to research the color amber, I discovered in the book of Ezekiel that Ezekiel, too, had encounters with God in which he experienced this same hue. Although the word "amber" is only used three times in the Old Testament and is of uncertain derivation[69] (meaning no one really knows where the word came from or has a point of reference to help define it), I have come to know this color as God's glory.

Out of the midst of the fire, burning with an amber glow, the four living creatures proceeded. The same four living creatures are mentioned in Revelation chapter four. In that chapter, we see that they are actually in the throne room in the presence of God. And we know that His glory fills the temple. So, when they marched out of the amber glow in Ezekiel's vision, they were coming from that place of glory.

Another time I was in corporate worship and we were singing in the Spirit. I began to sing one beautiful note. I couldn't get away from it. As I kept singing it, the Lord clearly spoke to me, "The note you're singing is the color green." It was as if I was experiencing Him in this green-sound color. My spirit eyes opened even more. This particular experience is actually quite hard to explain. It was as if God was connecting a musical sound with a color and revealed to me that the two had a corresponding relationship. I later read that some in the scientific community have proposed that there is a connection between sound and color. This is also what some in the field of psychology may call *synesthesia*.[70] But in the Kingdom, it's an invitation to learn that God is incredibly intentional and everything He does is with purpose and has astounding connection!

There are no anomalies in heaven. We can experience God in super-natural ways, ways beyond the natural world, if we allow our logical minds to rest and our spirits to soar. Sometimes, the revelation of what He shows us comes immediately. Other times it unfolds as we meet with Him in the secret place and He gives us revelation layer by layer. Being in a community of believers who shares these types of experiences can also help with understanding.

Definitions

When you see a color in the Spirit, ask the Lord what it represents. As you build your own dictionary, He may give you a personalized interpretation. There are, of course, some commonly held definitions or meanings for colors, some offered in the context of a passage using the rule of first mention.

Here are just a few:[71]

- **Blue** – Revelation, Holy Spirit

- **Red** – The blood of Jesus, love

- **White** – Purity, holiness

- **Green** – New life, growth

- **Brown** – Humanity

- **Black** – Mysteries of God, mortality

I'm intentionally not providing an exhaustive list so you can seek more colors out on your own, whether that be with the Holy Spirit, friends, or the vast array of resources available.

Prophetic Numbers and Repetitions

Besides impressions, feelings, dreams, and visions, God uses many other ways to get our attention and invite us into dialogue on a matter. "Repetition" is what I call one of these languages. Have you ever, for some reason, kept seeing the same thing over and over, like a butterfly or moving truck? Or do you see numbers in succession and repetition like 111, 222, 333, or 444? This is yet another language of the Spirit in which He highlights or emphasizes things to get our attention. When you keep seeing the same thing repeatedly (and I would suggest, without trying to find it, it finds you), God is inviting you into a conversation.

"Call on me in prayer and I will answer you. I will show you great and mysterious things which you still do not know about." (NET) – Jeremiah 33:3

Did you notice the Scripture address there? 333! Did you see the Scripture address on this chapter cover page? 222! God is inviting us into mysteries constantly. All we have to do is become more aware. What I love about these two verses is that God is using the language of repetition in His Word to help us define and discover the very mysteries He talks about! If we want to know more about mysteries, all we need to do is talk with Him...and He *will* reveal the deep and hidden things. That's a promise. It's often in this place of intimacy that God prophetically speaks to us about a situation or circumstance in which He wants to demystify revelation so we can apply it in very practical ways.

I often see a host of repetitions: numbers, words, animals, insects, bumper stickers, nations, etc. When I do, I know that He's drawing me in closer on a matter. Ever since I was a kid, I have seen numbers in repetition. In fact, numbers were probably the first thing in repetition I can significantly remember in my relationship with God.

In elementary school, I would see 10:01 often on the clock. Unfortunately, with a lack of teaching or understanding, my experience was surrounded with fear. In my unhealed little mind, it meant something ominous. I'd try to avoid it, but when I'd see it, for some reason, there was a peace and clarity I couldn't reconcile. I knew it was significant (discernment), but I didn't know why.

For a long while in life, the repetitions stopped. When I was about 30 years old, I started seeing the number 649 all the time. So much so that it scared me. Yet, at the same time I was really intrigued. Finally, one day, after seeing it for what seemed to be the thousandth time (again, without looking for it), I said, "Okay, Lord, you have my attention." That's one of the best things you can say to God.

One day, after a month or more of seeing 649 all over the place, I got a message from my hair stylist. She said she was calling to confirm my appointment and asked that I call her if I couldn't make it. She followed this up by saying, "Please call me at xxx-0649." Immediately, my spirit leapt as I knew this was why God had been showing me the number! I started to pray for her like crazy, as did my mom. My stylist, at that time, was into numerology and seeking psychics for life direction, as she was close to divorce from her husband. Although, sadly, they did end up divorcing, she came to know the Lord several years later and now her grown daughter and husband are pastors on staff at church! It was incredibly exciting to see all this play out in the natural. I knew God had invited me to be a part of her salvation, if only a small part of partnering with Him, so she could get to know Him as her Savior and Friend!

After the revelation of 649, the repetitions from the Lord began to expand and increase. At times when I saw a repeated number, I felt God was just saying that He loved me. Other times, I knew He was inviting me into a matter that He deeply cared about. The number 649 gave way to other numbers, all of which were invitations into things the Lord wanted to share with me and to draw me into partnering with Him in some way.

Years later, as I was leading a group of people, I started to see 10:01 again. I hardly had to ask the Lord what it meant. I always come so alive when I'm leading people, especially when I'm leading them in a teaching capacity. I knew instinctively that He was saying I was walking in destiny, living in the fullness of what He had created me to do! All those years when I was young, He was with me. He was telling me that He never left me or forsook me. In fact, in Ecclesiastes 3:11, as we've seen in this manual, it says that He places eternity in our hearts. All those years, He was depositing eternity into the place of my heart that would one day resonate with confidence that He does in fact know the plans He has for us and they are plans to prosper us and not harm us, plans to give us hope for the amazing future He already sees!

Definitions

There are some commonly held meanings for Biblical numbers. In fact, there is a whole field of study to define and understand numbers in the Bible, especially as it relates to the Hebrew Bible.

Here are some numbers and their meanings to get you started on your journey of understanding this language of the Spirit:[72]

- **One** – The beginning of something

- **Two** – A witness

- **Three** – The Godhead

- **Four** – Creation

- **Five** – Grace

- **Six** – Humanity, man

- **Seven** - Godly perfection

- **Twelve** – God's government

Do you ever look at the clock and see 10:10 or 11:11? When a number is repeated twice it can mean there's a heavenly witness to what God's showing you. Remember, the number *two* can mean "witness." God can also show us numbers in sequence like 444 or 555. When I see a number in sequence three times, like 444, it's as if the Lord is saying the Godhead (Father, Son, and Holy Spirit) are really emphasizing a spiritual reality and bearing witness to it, as well. "What spiritual reality?" you might ask. Well, it depends on the circumstances in which He shows me. Sometimes when He shows me a number, it can correlate to a Scripture address, like Daniel 2:22 or Jeremiah 33:3, or it can be a new revelation. I always tell our students, however, don't rely on what He told you last week or on commonly held interpretations, solely. When He shows you something, ask Holy Spirit! He might surprise you with a fresh, personalized revelation that speaks directly to your life circumstances.

Other Examples of Repetitions

- I had begun to see the "Coexist" bumper sticker everywhere I went, on practically every car. I had no idea why the Lord kept showing me the bumper sticker, at first. I pressed in time after time. Finally, I felt like the Lord gave me the answer. The concept of "coexist," as you may know, is for peace and unity among all peoples and religions. But how many of you know there is only One Prince of Peace, only One King of kings and Lord of lords? There is no real peace apart from Jesus. The philosophy behind religious coexistence is based in humanism and promotes the belief that all religions are equal and should peacefully dwell together on the earth, with one no greater than the other. The Lord told me that whenever I saw this bumper sticker, I was to declare, "Jesus, You are Lord of all. You are exalted above everything on this earth. You are the only real Peace people will ever know." God showed me that the humanistic declarations of this earth must be replaced by heavenly declarations, to exalt Jesus and tear down strongholds. To this day, whenever I see this bumper sticker, I make the declaration, "God, you are exalted above all else. There is only One way to you and that's Jesus. He is the King of all kings and Lord of all lords."

- For a season, the Canadian National Anthem kept going around in my head. Within the span of a few days, I kept seeing "Canada" everywhere: maple leaves, the Canadian flag, and even heard people talking about Canada. I asked the Lord and didn't get an instant answer, so I began to intercede for Canada. In a situation like this, it can be helpful to see what the current news is in a nation that God highlights to you. It may give additional insight or prayer points. When I don't get specific direction, I lift Him up over the nation and intercede as the Spirit leads.

- I was going through a difficult period of transition. Transition for me can often be very uncomfortable as the fulfilled prophetic promise seemingly waits through a period of personal transformation. Usually, it looks like faulty internal beliefs colliding with the Word of God. I get invited into a renewing-of-the-mind process. If you can't tell by the diplomatic wording here, personal transformation is painful! Ugh. I was desperate to know God's heart for me in this season because I was really struggling with the waiting. Being out in nature is very life-giving to me. It always has been. In fact, I often feel like I can hear God more clearly when I'm outside in the sun, listening to the birds and the sounds of the day. It was a beautiful season in Arizona, one in which you could be outside for prolonged periods of time, and I would sit in the backyard and talk with God. Over the span of many days, what looked like a big Monarch butterfly would flutter past me. At first, I just enjoyed him flying around aimlessly amongst the other winged creatures. Then I realized God was talking. I positioned my heart to hear what He was saying. One afternoon, I took the trash out and the butterfly showed up. He followed me all the way to the trash bin! Right before he took off in a different direction (as they often do), he came over to my hand, landed on it, and flew away. It was like a kiss from the butterfly! I knew God was confirming my transformational season. He was telling me that this metamorphosis, like the caterpillar-to-butterfly, would result in a greater revelation of my identity as a daughter of the ultimate King (Monarch) and result in a new level of internal beauty. God is always preparing us for new levels of glory![73]

Sometimes the Lord will bring understanding immediately to a symbol He shows you. Sometimes it will unfold over years. Be patient, but be persistent. Don't forget what He shows you. Steward the revelation by writing it down and dialoguing with Him. Sometimes He might not give you the interpretation right away or even reveal the outcome *of* the mystery He's inviting you into. When He shows you a nation, like my Canada experience, it may just be to partner with Him in intercession. Lean in. Ask Him how He would like you to pray. You may not know until you get to heaven the impact of your prayers, but you can know that your fervent prayers will result in much fruit![74]

Reflection

1. What colors have you experienced in the Spirit? _____

_____

2. What interpretations/meanings do you have for those colors? _____

_____

3. What numbers do you see often? _____

_____

4. What insight do you have on them? _____

_____

5. What other repetitions have you experienced? _____

_____

Activation

Activation #1

Use the chart below to find Biblical meaning for numbers and colors. Then, ask the Holy Spirit to give you revelation so that you can continue to build your dictionary.

Number	Scripture	Meaning/Definition
1		
2		
3		
4		
5		
6		
7		
8		
9		
10		
11		
12		

24		
50		
120		

Color	Scripture	Meaning/Definition
Red/Scarlett		
Black		
White		
Brown		
Blue		
Amber		
Green		
Purple		
Gold		
Silver		

Activation #2

Spend some time with the Holy Spirit and ask Him for definitions for the following symbols:

What could the number 411 mean?

_____

What could the number 911 mean?

_____

What could the color pink represent?

_____

What could the color yellow represent?

_____

Dreams

"In a dream, in a vision of the night, when deep sleep falls upon men, while slumbering on their beds, then He opens the ears of men, and seals their instruction."
(NKJV)
Job 33:15-16

Our walk with God is a life of invitation. When He speaks to us through the many languages of the Spirit, He is inviting us to occupy a greater place in His world. Although not every dream we have is from God, dreams are one of the languages He uses to talk with us. Often, we can be so busy throughout the day that we aren't tuned in to the still, small voice of God. One way of getting our attention and depositing eternity in our hearts is through our dream life. The passage below gives us insight into why God speaks to us through the language of dreams.

"In a dream, in a vision of the night, when deep sleep falls upon men, while slumbering on their beds, then He opens the ears of men, and seals their instruction. In order to turn man from his deed, and conceal pride from man, He keeps back his soul from the Pit, and his life from perishing by the sword." (NKJV)

Job 33:15-18

God gives us dreams at night to help us. Sometimes the dreams He gives us are full of instruction and revelation. He is a good dad who cares a lot about His kids. He will talk to us in dreams to stave off eminent danger. Sometimes He gives us dreams to save us from ourselves. He doesn't want us to go down a path of destruction, as indicated in the above passage. Proverbs 14:12, in fact, says that there is a way that seems right to a man, but in the end it leads to death. Additionally, John 6:63 tells us that the flesh profits us nothing. When we don't cultivate a relationship with the Spirit we don't realize that He's the only One who gives life. Nothing else will bring us to the fullness of destiny than the Spirit of God. Not our good ideas, plans, or programs. Now, these things can definitely be inspired by and given to us by God, but sometimes we get our eyes off Jesus and onto our own abilities. God wants to keep us from the deeds of the flesh and our propensity to gloat in anything we feel originated with us.

Dreams are one of the languages that God uses to equip us for the amazing and unique destiny that He's placed within us. This particular language, however, requires a bit more experience and understanding before we can often apply it to our lives, in that it is primarily communicated through symbolism and the fact that not all dreams are from God.

Glimpses of Destiny

As we delve into the language of dreams, read through the following passage and note anything that stands out to you.

"At Gibeon the Lord appeared to Solomon…and God said, "Ask for whatever you want me to give you." Solomon answered, "You have shown great kindness to your servant, my father David, because he was faithful to you and righteous and upright in heart. You have continued this great kindness to him and have given him a son to sit on his throne this very day. "Now, Lord my God, you have made your servant king in place of my father David. But I am only a little child and do not know how to carry out my duties. Your servant is here among the people you have chosen, a great people, too numerous to count or number. So give your servant a discerning heart to govern your

people and to distinguish between right and wrong. For who is able to govern this great people of yours?" The Lord was pleased that Solomon had asked for this. So God said to him, "Since you have asked for this and not for long life or wealth for yourself, nor have asked for the death of your enemies but for discernment in administering justice, I will do what you have asked. I will give you a wise and discerning heart, so that there will never have been anyone like you, nor will there ever be. Moreover, I will give you what you have not asked for—both wealth and honor—so that in your lifetime you will have no equal among kings." (NIV)

1 Kings 3:5-13

Had you been previously familiar with this passage? Growing up in the church and hearing many sermons, I certainly was. Did you know this entire interaction happened in a *dream*? I was shocked to find that out! Sometimes our dream life can be obscure and it's hard to understand what they mean. But real encounters with God can happen in dreams! The Hebrew word for dream here is the word *chalowm*, which can mean a prophetic dream.[75] God can speak to us prophetically at night. He talks to us about our future and destiny. God visited Solomon to not only see what was in his heart, but to deposit within him what he needed for his God-designed future and a promise of the riches and honor he didn't even ask for!

As we look more closely, we can see some amazing principles in this passage:

1. **God can interact with us in dreams.**

God is not limited in the number of ways He can speak with us. One way He speaks is through dreams and these can be real interactions with Him!

2. **God dreams are prophetic in nature.**

Often when God talks to us in dreams, it's to prepare us for our future. He is depositing within our spirits the tools and revelation we need to carry out our destiny. God is so good. He's always preparing and equipping us.

3. **Solomon had a history with God.**

He knew that God had been faithful to his dad, David, and that gave him a marker, a point from which to place his trust. He essentially said, "God was faithful to my dad, David, and He will be faithful to me." It's important for us to build a history with God so that when times get tough, we can anchor ourselves to Him, knowing that He has never failed us.

4. **Solomon knew there were keys to experiencing God's lovingkindness.**

Solomon knew that because his dad, David, walked before God displaying the character traits of faithfulness, righteousness, and integrity, God's great and faithful love was made manifest. These same character traits can help us in experiencing God's goodness, as well.

5. Solomon asked for the right thing.

Have you ever wondered how Solomon knew to ask for the right thing from God? I would suggest he was already cultivating the seeds of wisdom and honor in his heart. Jesus said that from out of the heart the mouth speaks.[76] In the dream, Solomon was not consciously conversing with God because he was asleep. So, this indicates that the condition of his heart was like his dad David's, full of righteousness and integrity. His spirit's response to God in the dream was a reflection of what was already within his heart. God knows the degree of increase we're ready for by the nature of our asking.

6. Wisdom is a key to abundance.

Solomon didn't ask for riches or wealth. He asked for discernment to administer justice. He knew that governing God's people was impossible without God's help. He also knew that God was his ultimate source *for* wisdom. As a result, God said He would give Solomon what he didn't ask for, riches and wealth! God was essentially telling Solomon that ruling with a heart of wisdom was an extension of God's own heart. It pleased the Lord so much that Solomon's heart was in the right place that He told him He would lavish Solomon with greater riches than anyone on the earth, ever! That's how much God cares that we lead people with His character.

7. Justice is important to God.

While mercy triumphs over judgment,[77] we still have governmental leaders who must rule in matters of fairness and righteousness. Justice is important to God. Righteousness and justice are the very foundation of His throne.[78] God is looking for people who will humble themselves to receive His wisdom and instruction so they can govern with the heart of heaven. He's looking for people who won't rely on earthly wisdom, but seek Him. He doesn't want people to rule with selfish agenda or a heavy hand, but a healthy heart like King Jesus. These people are prime candidates to rule governments and nations!

The Lord made good on the promises He made to Solomon in this dream encounter. He not only prepared and equipped Solomon for an amazing destiny, He gave him so much wisdom and wealth that the Queen of Sheba was "overwhelmed" by the display, gave Solomon more riches, and worshipped God (see 1 Kings 10)!

Dreams in the Bible

Let's take a walk through the Bible and look at some of the people who experienced God through this language of dreams and some principles they offer for us today. This isn't an exhaustive list, but it will give you a good overview of how God uses the language of dreams.

1. Abimelech

In Genesis 20:1-7 we see that Abraham lied about his wife Sarah. They were staying in a new region during their travels to the land where God would fulfill his destiny and Abraham thought they would surely get killed. So, he offered up his wife to Abimelech, saying she was his sister, in hopes that they wouldn't die. Can you believe that!? Saying your wife is your sister to save your own life? Wow. Well, God couldn't either, so He visited Abimelech in a dream and said, "You are as good as dead because of the woman you have taken; she is a married woman." (NIV) Abimelech responded to God, *in the dream,* and said, "Lord, will you destroy an innocent nation? Did he not say to me, 'She is my sister,' and didn't she also say, 'He is my brother?' I have done this with a clear conscience and clean hands." God acknowledged that Abimelech's conscience was clear and said He wouldn't destroy him if he returned Sarah to Abraham.

In this passage, we see God give someone a *warning* in a dream. This someone was also a "non-believer." God speaks to people who don't yet know Him! Abimelech's dream was most likely an *encounter* and both *prophetic* and *directional* in nature.

2. Jacob

Turn to Genesis 28:10-17 and read about the dream encounter Jacob had with God. In this dream, Jacob experienced the atmosphere of heaven, with angels ascending and descending from heaven to earth. God spoke to Jacob in this *prophetic* dream and gave him a very similar promise to what He'd given his grandfather, Abraham, in Genesis 22. There's an interesting principle to draw from this dream: God gives us generational promises! I wonder how many promises the Lord has given each of us through our family lines that are still waiting to be discovered and revived? How many generational inheritances ready to be reclaimed?

3. Joseph

If you're familiar with any dreamers in the Bible, there's a good chance you know Joseph. In Genesis 37, we see his story unfold. First, Joseph was already hated by his brothers because he was Jacob's favorite son. To make matters worse, Joseph, in his immaturity, bragged to his brothers about two significant dreams he had in which all of his brothers were bowing down to him. Not smart. As a result, his brother's hatred towards him grew and they, eventually, plotted to kill him. They were just short of succeeding. Joseph's life story is one of my favorites in the Bible. As we continue to read about his life's journey, we get a glimpse into the many character trials he endured. I don't necessarily love character trials, but I do love how God will refine us, if we allow Him to, to prepare us for high positions of authority, where His purposes will be fulfilled! What an honor.

Joseph was bought by Potiphar and grew in favor with his Egyptian master. Resisting advances by Potiphar's wife and her lying about it, though, Joseph was imprisoned. In prison, God's favor continued to rest on Joseph. He helped two men by interpreting dreams that troubled them, stating, "Do not interpretations belong to God? Tell me your dreams." He successfully interpreted the dreams and, as a result, was remembered when Pharaoh had a dream that no wise man in his court could interpret. After not only successfully interpreting Pharaoh's dreams (stating again that he couldn't do it, but God could), he aided Pharaoh by suggesting solutions that would help him prepare for the famine the dreams foretold. Pharaoh, knowing that God's wisdom rested on Joseph, appointed him governor in Egypt, only second in command to Pharaoh himself. The famine was, indeed, severe. Jacob told his sons to go to Egypt to get grain so they wouldn't die. His brothers did as their father had said and arrived in Egypt. At the feet of the governor, unknowingly their brother Joseph, they came and bowed down (Genesis 42:6).

Joseph was a dreamer, with not only an active dream life, but the gift from God to interpret dreams. The dreams Joseph had when he was a young man did prove to be *prophetic* dreams about the significance and reality of his future. Both of the dreams about his brothers bowing down to him had *symbolic* language with a *literal* application. It's interesting to note that Abraham, considered a prophet by God, had an encounter with God as he was sleeping, Isaac had encounters with God, Jacob experienced God in dreams, and it's recorded that Joseph had an incredibly active dream life. Again, we see a generational inheritance down the family line of Abraham.

4. Gideon

In Judges 7, God gives Gideon confidence to go to war with a little 300-man army. After causing his army to dwindle from 33,000 to 300, God then tells Gideon to go to the Midianite camp one night. God instructed him to take his servant if he was afraid and that Gideon would be strengthened by what he would observe. With his servant, he went spying on the men. As they were there, no doubt in the shadows, Gideon overhears one warrior tell another about a dream he had. He dreamt that a loaf of barley bread rolled down the hill into the valley where the Midianite camp was. The bread struck a tent and the tent fell down. Amazingly, the other warrior who was listening to his fellow compadre tell the dream, has the interpretation! He turns to his friend and says, "Dude, the barley loaf is Gideon. God's favor rests on him and we're all gonna die." That's not verbatim, but it's pretty close. Overhearing the dream and its interpretation, Gideon gets the assurance he needs to lead the tiny army to victory. This dream was a *prophetic*, *symbolic* dream.

5. Daniel

As I mentioned in the chapter on visions, Daniel is one of my favorite people in the Bible (as you can see, I actually have lots of favorites). Daniel, like Joseph, was in a whole other league. Daniel was an Israelite and was used by God to interpret dreams for kings. He gave himself to fasting and prayer and, as result, had a remarkable life filled with all kinds of God encounters.

In Daniel chapter 2, we see that King Nebuchadnezzar had a dream that troubled him. He called all his magicians and wise men to interpret the dream, but wouldn't tell them what the dream was. He demanded that they tell *him* the dream. How's that for testing the authenticity of your magicians? Of course, we know that they weren't able to do what the king requested. Daniel, primed by God to take the stage, asked if he could have some time to try and interpret the dream. It's interesting to note that the king wouldn't give the enchanters any time at all, stating that they'd be chopped to pieces and their houses burned to the ground. But he granted Daniel time. It's evident God's favor was resting on Daniel to influence influencers. God wants to use us to give divine counsel and interpret dreams of kings and people in high places of authority, too! Daniel went and told his three Israelite friends so they could seek God with him. We all need friends who will seek God with us on certain matters. That night, the interpretation came to Daniel in a vision. He went to King Nebuchadnezzar and declared, "No wise man, medium, diviner, or astrologer is able to make known to the king the mystery he has asked about. But there is a God in heaven who reveals mysteries, and He has let King Nebuchadnezzar know what will happen in the last days." He then was able to give King Nebuchadnezzar the dream *and* the interpretation.

Not only did Daniel interpret dreams, in Daniel chapter 7 we see that he had a *prophetic, symbolic* dream about the end of times. What I love about Daniel is that he lead a life of consecration to the Lord and God invited him into eternal mysteries and secrets. Daniel was an intimate with God and God knew that He could trust him. Although the dream Daniel had was terrifying to him because of the violence in the earth he saw in the dream, God gave Daniel a glimpse of the end: God's kingdom being established in the earth, by the authority of Jesus through His sons and daughters. That's us!

Let's briefly go to the New Testament.

6. Joseph

Let's admit, it would be very hard to commit to marriage knowing the woman you love is pregnant...and not by you. Joseph decided he wanted to secretly divorce Mary. The scandal of her impregnation was too much for him and he wanted to protect her from the embarrassment of a public separation. In Matthew 1:20 it says, "But after he had considered this, an angel of the Lord appeared to him in a dream and said, 'Joseph son of David, do not be afraid to take Mary home as your wife, because what is conceived in her is from the Holy Spirit.'" (NIV) I bet if anyone found themselves in this situation, they too would need a heavenly sign! This dream was an *encounter* offering *encouragement* as a word of wisdom and was *directional* in nature.

After Jesus was conceived, there was immediate and imminent danger over His life. Back in those days, they didn't have cell phones or social media. So, God sent another angel in a dream to deliver an urgent message to Joseph. "When they had gone (the wise men), an angel of the Lord appeared to Joseph in a dream. 'Get up,' He said, 'take the child and his mother and escape to Egypt. Stay there until I tell you, for Herod is going to search for the child to kill him (Matthew 2:13 parenthesis added).'" To protect baby Jesus, God sent an angel in an *encounter* dream to give Joseph a *warning*. This dream was also *directional* in nature. Once the threat was gone, an angel appeared to Joseph again, "After Herod died, an angel of the Lord appeared in a dream to Joseph in Egypt saying, 'Get up! Take the child and his mother and go to the land of Israel because those who sought the child's life are dead (Matthew 2:19-20).'"

7. Pilate's Wife

In Matthew 27, Jesus stood in front of the governor, Pilate, and was questioned about all the accusations from the chief priests, elders and people. While His accusers were shouting out their claims, Jesus was silent. Pilate was amazed by Jesus' composure and refusal to defend himself. Unfortunately, Pilate bowed to peer pressure. He asked the church leaders who they wanted to release, a notorious prisoner or Jesus. While he was still deliberating, his wife communicated with him: "While Pilate was sitting on the judge's seat, his wife sent him this message: "Don't have anything to do with that innocent man, for I have suffered a great deal today in a dream because of him (NIV – verse 19)." God warned Pilate through a dream his wife had that Jesus' blood would be on his hands if he turned him over to the Jews to be crucified. This *prophetic warning* dream (coming as a word of wisdom) was to aid in Pilate's decision. He, however, did not heed it.

Dream Basics[79]

Now that we've covered a handful of spiritual dreams with Biblical precedent, let's go over some dream basics. This may be review for you, but it will help us lay a foundation for the next chapter: Dream Interpretation.

- There are three sources of dreams: God, the enemy, and ourselves.

- Most dreams we have are from ourselves and about ourselves.

- As we saw at the beginning of the chapter, God uses dreams to bypass our consciousness so that He can deposit destiny and instruction.

- A good indicator if the dream is about you is if you are the main subject of the dream. If you are first person, the dream is most likely about you.

- If you are more of an observer in the dream, it is most likely about an external circumstance.

- Most dreams are symbolic, not literal. This is why Pharaoh and Nebuchadnezzar, for instance, needed an interpretation.

- Our dream life usually has ebbs and flows. We may go through seasons where we don't dream much at all, seasons where it doesn't seem like we even sleep because of the overflow of dreams, and seasons where God uses dreams to speak to our hearts.

- Stewarding your dreams can lead to an increased understanding of symbolism and metaphoric language.

- Continue to develop your dictionary with the Lord, as He may have a new meaning for a symbol in your dream!

- Purity of heart and taking care of our physical bodies can help prevent negative dreams.

Soul Dreams

Most dreams that we have are about ourselves. Often these dreams can be intense and full of symbolism, but once we have a few key pieces of information on the basics of dreams, we can begin the journey of understanding and interpreting them.

- Soul dreams can be about stress or anxiety, the condition of our soul, or generally processing life. Although these dreams may not be as exciting as a prophetic dream from God, they can provide a lot of insight, a gauge, into the state of our hearts.

- These dreams can be intense with a wide range of emotions and feelings.

- These dreams aren't usually very colorful. They tend to be more subdued colors or grey.

- Sometimes these dreams can be confused with demonic dreams because of the intensity of actions and emotions.

One of the most terrifying dreams I've had was *not* a demonic dream. At the time, it certainly felt so. We can often dismiss "bad" dreams thinking they're from the enemy, but that's not always the case. Dreams give us a tremendous amount of understanding about the condition of our soul. I was going through a major season of breakthrough in life, determined to not let any issues within me get in the way of my destiny. One night I dreamt that I was walking in a house with my sister (the new creation me). She was carrying a big glass jar with water (emotions) and two fish in it. We walked past a door that lead to the basement (my subconscious) towards the kitchen (place of transition) and, suddenly, a man (my old/flesh man) came out from the basement. His eyes were huge and looked crazed. As he came out of the pitch black into the room, he walked very methodically and slowly over to me. I took my sister by the arm and led her calmly to the back door and said, "It's going to be okay. Go get help." I turned back to the man. He had a hypodermic needle filled with a clear substance. He slowly flicked it to get the air out. He came over to me and grabbed my right hand (spiritual authority or my ability to grasp what God was doing) and injected the needle between my thumb and first finger. I knew he was trying to kill me. As he did this, I said, "Jesus, take care of this for me." And the dream ended.

I woke up immediately. I was freaked out and my hand physically hurt in the place where the crazy man injected the needle, *in my dream*! After I calmed down and processed the dream, I knew that the man was my "old man," my flesh. My old man was so used to being in control and "he" was ticked off that he was losing territory in my life, territory that he'd had control of for a long time. When the feelings of this dream subsided, a few days went by, and I fully processed it, I realized this was actually a *positive* dream, though it hardly felt like it at the time.

Another important key for understanding dreams is to pay attention to recurring dreams. Recurring dreams are a way that God highlights or emphasizes things that very important. I had a recurring dream for years that I was cheating on my husband. I would always feel so terrible when I woke up. I would freak out and pray, "God, is this really in my heart?" I've never cheated on my husband in real life and, with God's grace, never will.

Finally, one night it all came together. I had a dream that I was in a construction worksite trailer at a new housing development. This good-looking guy was trying to flirt with me and I said, "Hey, look, I know that you're good-looking and all but I'm married," and I walked out of the trailer. Outside, I walked toward the frames of new houses and the sun was rising over the development. The dream ended.

When I woke up, I *immediately* knew the meaning of the dream. My "husband" in the dream was Jesus! I was cheating on Him with my time and activities throughout the day. When the sun rose over the housing development, I knew it meant that a new day had dawned in my person and that Jesus had taken a new priority in my life.

Spiritual Dreams[80]

Spiritual dreams do not originate with us. They can come from either God or the enemy.

Dreams from God

As stated in this manual, all of life with God is a life of invitation. Revelation 3:20 says, "Listen! I stand at the door and knock. If anyone hears My voice and opens the door, I will come in to him and have dinner with him, and he with Me." While this verse is commonly referred to as a salvation verse, it gives us insight into God's nature. He's not pushy. He knocks and waits. He invites. It's the same with dreams He gives us. He's inviting us into mystery. Jeremiah 33:3 says, "Call to Me and I will answer you and tell you great and incomprehensible things you do not know." Whatever mystery He invites us into, He promises to give us understanding.

Let's take a peek at some characteristics of God-given dreams.

- Dreams from God are usually, but not always, packed with brilliant color!

- God dreams usually feel full of amazement and awe. These dreams can be very exciting.

- These dreams are usually prophetic in nature, in that they are revealing the future.

- These dreams can either be about us or external things, like people or places.

- God dreams can be about our call and destiny.

- Dreams from God can, among other things, be directional, correctional, instructional, full of encouragement, insight, and/or Divine revelation.

- Dreams about external things, like people for instance, can be a call to intercession.

Instructional Dreams

I had a dream where a female (Holy Spirit) and I were talking. She had a two-page, stapled, 8 ½ x 11 document and turned it around on the desk so I could see it. She said something like, "This is what you need to know in order to pray for Israel." It had a logo in the upper left hand corner that was blue and white, like the Israeli flag. After I woke up, I spent time with the Lord and asked Him about the dream. He showed me how to pray for Israel by directing me in Scripture and reminding me of a vision I had prior to the dream (it's good to note here that God connected dots between a vision and a dream I had, which my stewarding of both aided).

Insight Dreams

I had a dream I was with one of my really good female friends. I turned to her and said, "Some pursue significance, but it's better to pursue humility." She replied, "I know what that means." In my time with the Lord after the dream, I wrote in my journal, "I think the Holy Spirit is going to continue teaching me about going low." God knows what we need for each season of life. He continually equips us, in advance, preparing us for our destiny and call. Ironically, humility is a key to promotion.[81]

Intercession/Warning Dreams

Some dreams are an invitation for intercession. These "God dreams" may not necessarily feel amazing or full of brilliant color, but God is wanting to show us something, preveniently, so we can partner with Him for a Kingdom outcome. Although these dreams may not feel awesome, they can still be spiritual and prophetic in nature.

My husband was interviewing for a job with a telecommunications company in the natural. One night, I had a dream that I was in a college union and a man was stealing from a telecommunications kiosk. From across the union, I yelled at him to stop. He turned around and threw a combination lock at my head from across the building. I ducked to dodge the lock. The dream ended.

A few days later, my husband told me that he should hear that day if he got the job. As the day went on, the representative from the company and my husband played phone tag. They just couldn't seem to connect. I sat on the couch and turned my attention to the Lord. He reminded me of the dream and I got an impression that He wanted me to pray against the "thief of the job." I took authority over miscommunication and declared they would connect by phone, in the Name of Jesus. My husband got the job that afternoon.

I had another intercession dream one night. In the dream, a man appeared to me and said, "Follow me." He said this three times throughout the dream. As I was following him, we got onto a ski lift-type ride and rode over a populated city. The ride stopped over a dilapidated building. On the second story was a massive sign that read, "Foster Care Tragedies and Traumas." This man and I dropped into the run-down building near a small group of people who were praying, my heart was warmed towards them. I walked outside, looked out at the city, and reflected. I said to myself in the dream, "I could fast for this cause once a month." Shortly after, the dream ended.

When I awoke, I knew that I had an invitation from the Lord to fast and intercede for the foster care and child protection system in the state I was living in, Arizona. Within a short period of having the dream, it was announced on the news that there was a newly-elected governor of the state and this governor would be overhauling the child protection agency, including giving it a new name!

Destiny Dreams

I had a significant dream in January 2014 where God revealed my call. The dream was so exciting and seemed too good to be true. In the dream, He gave me insight into three keys of the call. When I woke up, I almost didn't write them down because the call seemed too awesome. Those keys have since given me the confidence and security to move forward with my destiny.

Teaching is a big part of what I'm called to, as well. Throughout my dream journey, I've had many dreams where I'm teaching people how to do things in the Spirit, how to move in the Spirit, how to do warfare, what the Kingdom of heaven is like, how to partner with the Lord, and dreams where I teach people how to hear God's voice. In 2010, I had a dream that I told someone, "God is always talking. All you have to do is tune in like a radio." I saw a knob, turned it, and made a sound like you're tuning the radio through static until a station comes in. The dream ended. I am now in a position where I teach people often. It's one of my joys in life to teach people about the Kingdom of God and how to hear His voice for themselves. In fact, I used this same radio analogy in the introduction to the manual you're holding in your hands!

Directional Dreams

Directional dreams can help us avoid mistakes or danger, or aid us in decision-making. God really wants to help us make great decisions! He never leaves us unequipped. The problem is, we can get so busy in life that we don't hear Him talking or we can be so determined to do our own thing we bulldoze past the still, small voice.

During one season, I had a big life decision to make. I had a dream that I made a certain choice which lead to trouble. When I woke up, I found out our son had a dream that same night in which I was in prison. He said I was in a jail cell, but the door was unlocked. My husband had a dream the next night that was very similar to our son's! God gave my whole family dreams about the direction for my life so I would know that I was not to proceed with what I was considering. God cares so much about your future that He will give you (and even people around you) dreams to guide decision-making.

Grace Dreams

When we can't do something in our own human strength, God will equip us with supernatural tools to move forward, despite opposition or pain. At one point in life, someone I loved hurt me quite deeply. As a result, I carried unforgiveness in my heart for a couple years. One night I had a dream that a woman (Holy Spirit) approached me and told me how she had forgiven a person in her life who had done the same thing. When I woke up, I was inexplicably and supernaturally filled with grace to forgive the person who had hurt me several years prior.

Correctional Dreams

Remember my dream about cheating on my "husband?" You may not think that was a correctional dream, but the Word of God says that it's His kindness that leads us to repentance. God showed me through recurring dreams that I wasn't making Him a priority in my life. His correction is always full of love.

Dreams with Significant Spiritual Leaders

When a significant leader in the Body of Christ shows up in dreams, it can often be symbolic for God Himself. I had a dream once where a very well-known prophet in the Body was in a conference room with me. We were doing a "SWOT" assessment of the prophetic ministry on a whiteboard. In the business world, SWOT stands for *strengths, weaknesses, opportunities,* and *threats.* In this dream, God was telling me that He would be working with me to assess the health of the prophetic ministry in the Body of Christ and infuse His heart into teachings that would change paradigms about this gift.

Dreams of Divine Creativity and Ideas

God can give us downloads in dreams, answers to "unsolvable" problems, designs, ideas, and creations. For instance, I'm an artist and I love to paint. One night, I had a dream that people could jump into one of my paintings and go places in the Spirit. In the natural, a friend of mine asked me to do a painting for her. I painted what I saw in the dream. She told me she hung it above her bed so she could have encounters with God!

I love fashion. I used to love to practice fashion sketches and thought maybe one day I'd be involved in the fashion world. I had a dream one night of one of the most gorgeous blouses. I have never seen this design in the natural. I knew that God had given it to me, if that was something I chose to pursue.

Dreams of Mysteries and Riddles

Do you remember my 404 dream from the chapter on prophecy? In one particular season of life, I was asking God for wisdom in my prayer and journaling times. I had a dream one night and in the dream, there was a sign. The sign read, "404 _____ _____ _____." Coming from the technology industry when I worked in the business world, I immediately knew the blanks to mean "Page Not Found." Remember, God loves to speak our language. This message on the internet is commonly known as a "404 error." Knowing that I love mystery and a good challenge, God posed a riddle to me to seek out. I thought to myself, "Well, if it's 'Page Not Found', I'm gonna find this page." I went to my Bible and, lo and behold, on page 404 Solomon is asking God for wisdom (1 Kings 3)!

Literal Dreams

We can have literal dreams that play out in the natural but, as you can see, the bulk of dreams tend to be symbolic in nature. This is why experience in dream interpretation is so important, because they can rarely be taken at face value. I had a fun dream one night that I, honestly, don't know the point of other than God loves to delight my heart. In the dream I was wearing an argyle sweater. In the natural I didn't own an argyle sweater. The very next day after the dream, my family and I went to a clothing store to get our son some new clothes. I walked around with them for a while. My husband was sifting through racks of clothes when I heard him say, "Hey, you'd look really cute in this." He turned around with an argyle sweater in hand. Needless to say, I bought it!

Dreams from the enemy

Dreams from the enemy aren't fun. Most of the time, we call these nightmares. There are some commonalities and keys with these dreams to give insight into the source of them.

- Dreams from the enemy are usually very dark.

- They usually invoke very intense, scary, or bad feelings.

- Sometimes these dreams are a result of things we have allowed into our lives. Watching horror movies, for instance, can be an "open door" to the enemy.

- These dreams can be confused with intense soul dreams.

- God can redeem and even use these dreams to teach us.

Let me start off by saying I do tend to have some spiritual warfare dreams. These dreams can be scary and intense at times, but the Lord is inviting me to partner with Him to release His solutions. These dreams aren't from the enemy, they aren't nightmares, but they can be frightening. They are actually prophetic in nature in that God is showing me how the enemy is scheming and what he is intending to unleash. If I accept God's invitation, I can ward off the plan of the enemy through partnership with God! God has given us authority in Christ and He invites us to use that authority here on the earth to bind up the works of the enemy.

With this being said, nightmares do happen. If you have a bad dream, ask God about it. He wants to give you insight into the dream or the reason for the dream. Nothing can happen outside of His control, so He will show you what you need to do in order for these dreams to stop.

He may, however, be giving you revelation, so I'd recommend that you don't quickly dismiss a dream just because it was negative. I had a dream one night there was a hideous female demon that kept approaching me and my son (who was young in the dream). This demon had green skin and the most hideous face. Every time she would get close to me and my son I would sing, "Jesus, Jesus, Jesus, there's just something about that Name. Kings and kingdoms will all pass away, but there's something about that Name."[82] As I would sing, she would move back about five to six feet away. When she'd come close again, I'd start singing that song and she'd back away. At one point, I took hold of my son's hand (a facet of me), who had fear in his eyes, and I said, "This is about agreement. It's very important that you break agreement with her and she'll go away." The dream ended.

Although this dream was very disturbing, it was key. God was giving me insight, in a "scary" dream, about an agreement I had with the enemy. Agreements can be as simple as allowing fear to be in your life over God's perfect love.

Some negative dreams can actually be encounters or discernment of spiritual beings. One night, I had a dream of a disturbance in our house. This dream was incredibly freaky. The next morning I was talking with our son and found out he had a dream about a gigantic hairy spider that broke the roof open of our house into his room and said, "You destroyed my house, I'm going to destroy yours." He said it was terrifying.

I knew immediately there was demonic activity in our house that night. So, I asked him if there was anything that had happened recently that had scared him. He told me that a particular video game he started playing was scaring him. Now, I had made it a practice of screening all books, videos, music, games, etc. for our son but for some reason I hadn't with this video game. In talking with him, I found out there was this entity in the game that would, essentially, take people over and control them. I knew immediately this was an "open door" to the enemy. I repented, prayed and covered our precious son. I asked him what he thought the best course of action was and he said, "stop playing." The nightmares and disturbance didn't happen again. What's beautiful is that although I opened the door, the Lord, by His grace, allowed the experience so I could repent and take authority to restore peace in our home. Plus, my son and I learned more about dreams!

Bad dreams can also give us understanding of new level of authority in our lives. I had a dream one night where two female demons were approaching me in an outdoor setting. I said calmly, "I have authority in Christ, you must go." And they backed away. The dream ended. In the natural, I knew that I was beginning to understand, at a greater level, the authority that I had in Christ. It was becoming a part of my DNA.

Conclusion

As we set out to steward and interpret our dreams (which we'll discuss in the next chapter), it's good to know that we don't want to compartmentalize or categorize our dreams too much. Often a soul dream can flow into a God dream and then back into a soul dream. God can show us the state of our heart and the prophetic promise of growth and healing in the same dream. Watch for shifts and changes in the dream or changes in color or feelings. Additionally, we may label something a nightmare when it may actually have a very positive interpretation.

Dreams are one of the many languages of the Spirit that God can use to talk with us. As with all the languages, stewarding leads to increase. When we demonstrate that we have value for what He's showing us, He shows us more!

Reflection

1. Can we talk to God in dreams? Explain. _____

_____

2. How often do you dream? _____

_____

3. What are the three sources of dreams? _____

_____

4. How might God redeem a "bad" dream? _____

_____

Activation

Activation #1

Put a journal or recorder by your bed. Before you go to sleep, let God know you're available for God dreams. Write down or record any dreams you receive.

Activation #2

Expect to get revelation from God and continue to build your dictionary of symbols and metaphor for future reference.

Activation #3

Look up these passages, record the dreamer and what type of dream they had. Write down any insight the Lord gives you.

Scripture	Dreamer/Type of Dream	Insight
Genesis 20:1-7		
Genesis 28:10-17		
Genesis 31:24		
Genesis 37:3-11		
Judges 7:12-16		
Matthew 1:20		
Matthew 2:13		
Matthew 2:19		
Matthew 27:19		

Dream Interpretation

"Don't interpretations belong to God?"
Genesis 40:8b

My dad is one of the most gifted dream interpreters I know. When I have a dream and the interpretation is as clear as mud, I call him. As I begin to share, he always says, "Okay honey, tell me again." One of two things will happen: he will give me insight that the Holy Spirit reveals to him which I never in a million years would have thought of, or as I'm sharing the second time, I'll blurt out, "I get it!" He is so keen in knowing when to help interpret and when to the let the Holy Spirit interpret for me. It's interesting to note our generational inheritance, just like Joseph and his family line. I dream because my dad dreams, and my son dreams because I dream!

Generally speaking, I believe the best person to interpret your dreams is you. 1 Corinthians 2:11 says, "For who among men knows the concerns of man except the spirit of the man that is in him?" No one knows you like you do! As we're getting started in learning to interpret our dreams, there is absolutely nothing wrong with asking people to help us or give us their opinion. But ultimately, the interpretation that will have the most impact is the one that the Holy Spirit resonates within you.

My heart for this chapter is that you will be greater equipped to interpret your own dreams. I hope to open a greater understanding of your dream life and create a further passion in you to journal or record your dreams. Remember, stewardship leads to increase.

Dreams are another way that God invites us into deeper relationship with Him. He is ever looking for ways to draw us in and spend time with us. This is often why He uses symbols. He wants us to run to Him when there's a mystery He wants to reveal. When you dream, as with anything in life, talk with Him about it!

Dream Interpretation Pointers

Dream interpretation definitely takes experience, Holy Spirit insight, and skill. But there are some general pointers that can help us set about the business of interpreting our dreams.

- Ask the Holy Spirit to give you the interpretation of a dream.

- Most dreams are symbolic. As with the symbolic nature of visions, build your dictionary with the Lord to better get a grasp of what these pictures mean.

- Steward your dreams through journaling, typing out, or voice recording.

- Don't hold to all definitions of symbolism out there like they're the gospel truth. Ask Holy Spirit!

- Use wisdom in who you share with. Remember Joseph?

- While there are common definitions, there is no formula to interpretation.

- The rule of first mention can help us interpret symbols in dreams from a Biblical perspective.

- The sooner you write your dream down, the better chance you have in remembering details.

- The manifestation of some dreams, like destiny dreams, may not play out for many years. Be patient.

- Sometimes it's not necessary to interpret every single detail in a dream.

- Sometimes it's not necessary to interpret every single dream.

Getting Started with Dream Interpretation

Okay, so let's get started with the basics of dream interpretation. Remember, both Joseph and Daniel said that interpretation belongs to the Lord, so invite the Holy Spirit into your interpretation process!

It's also good to remember that a lot of dream interpretation starts with understanding metaphor and symbolism. A metaphor is defined as, "A figure of speech in which a term or phrase is applied to something to which it is not literally applicable in order to suggest a resemblance..."[83] Symbolism means, "The practice of representing things by symbols..." [84] An example of dream symbolism was Joseph's dream about the sun, moon, and stars bowing down to him. The celestial bodies didn't literally bow down to him, they were symbolic of his father, mother, and brothers.[85]

When we set out to interpret our dreams, it's good to remember that most of them aren't literal. This helps out tremendously when you have a dream about a co-worker who dies or moves to China. Do not call this co-worker and tell them you've had an ominous dream about them or that they should get their passport ready and sell everything they have! The dream may be about you. The interpretation of these two dream examples, respectively, may be death to your old self or God moving you into unknown, unfamiliar territory.

Although most dreams are metaphoric or symbolic in nature, they often have a real-life application. Joseph dreamt of sheaves of grain bowing down to him. Sheaves didn't literally bow down to him, his brothers did.[86] He had a *symbolic, prophetic* dream with a *literal* application. It's good to note that the manifestation of this dream didn't happen for about 20 years or so *after* he had the dream.

As you develop your dictionary and your understanding of dream language, you will begin to know more quickly if a dream is about you or someone else, if it's a soul dream or spirit dream, or if a dream should be dismissed or stewarded. God wants to develop a native language with you. Continuing to add to your dictionary is vital because the interpretation of a dream itself will most likely come from and resonate within you. God speaks your language! He may reveal things that only you would understand. This is why I love to give people tools to interpret their own dreams. I'll help them along for a while but, ultimately, I want them to learn to depend on God.

Interpreting Dreams

When I set out to interpret my own dream or help someone else interpret a dream, I ask a lot of questions. This great practice came from someone I see as an authority on dream interpretation: my dad! He has taught me so much about the interpretation of dreams. Namely, ask questions and listen. I've learned that this gives tremendous insight. It also allows the person to remember details, as they're recounting the dream.

One caveat: when helping people interpret dreams, as with the prophetic, we must use a heart of love. Dreams can be very revealing about where people are at in any area of life. When I'm teaching students about interpretation and going through a whiteboard exercise in class, I look for volunteers to share a dream that we can interpret together. Typically, I will give them several weeks' notice so they can plan ahead. However, I always warn them that dreams can be exposing and ask them to really think through whether they want to share publicly.

Using a heart of love when interpreting a dream for someone may mean considering surroundings, leaving part of the interpretation out until no one is around but the person themselves, or using softening language like, "I'm just submitting this to you for consideration...," Remember, love covers, it doesn't expose.

Additionally, when interpreting for someone else, I like to take the "I submit this to you approach" and not a "this is what you need to do approach." Like a prophetic word, we want to leave the application up to them and the Lord. Dream interpretation is not meant to be pastoral counsel.

Interpretation Keys

Here are some keys to dream interpretation:

- Pay attention to the things that get your attention. These items usually have significance.

- How did you *feel* in the dream? This can be one of the biggest keys to interpretation of the dream.

- Once you record the dream, repeat it or go through it again. This helps with a recollection of details.

- Were you the main person in the dream or were you more of an observer? Again, this can indicate source and subject matter. Remember, most dreams are about ourselves.

- Were there other people in your dream? These may be different facets of yourself or can indicate what these people *represent* to you. In other words, if you have a prophet in your dream, God may be speaking to you about the prophetic as it operates in your life, not literally about that particular person.

- Dreams within dreams or recurring dreams are significant. Ask God about them.

114

- God is creative and can use a play on words in dreams. If someone named Dawn shows up in your dream, it could mean a new day is dawning in your life! What are some plays on words you can think of?

- Were the colors in your dream rich and beautiful or more subdued or non-existent? This can be an indication of the source of the dream.

- Did the dream shift and change from one scene to another? If so, this may indicate the source of the dream has shifted.

- Significant events in your life can intensify dreams or the frequency of dreams. Stressors can also affect dreams.

- Think about a title for your dream. Often the title you give a dream can be a key to the interpretation.[87]

- Sometimes it's not necessary to interpret every single detail in a dream. What were the main things that stood out to you?

- Numbers, colors, words, and phrases can be very significant in dreams. Write them down immediately and research their meanings. And, of course, ask Holy Spirit!

- Have you been to a place in a dream multiple times? This happens to me with a certain airport in my dreams. This can be very significant. Ask God what He might be saying or emphasizing.

- For me, often a female or a person whose face I can't really see is the Holy Spirit. However, sometimes a female can be a demon. Other times, a female like my sister, may be a facet of myself. How you *felt* in the dream will give insight into who or what this person may represent. Often God shows up in my dreams as different leaders in the Body of Christ.

- Getting distance from the dream can help you interpret more objectively. Once the feelings have subsided, it can help you look at the dream more analytically as you interpret the symbols or it can help you connect with the Holy Spirit in a greater way, without the feelings of the dream clouding your thought.

- Sometimes the interpretation won't come for years! This is why stewarding is so important. I recently had a real-life circumstance in which the Holy Spirit reminded me of a dream I had *seven* years prior. This dream equipped me with tools for decision-making to navigate a very sensitive situation.

- Use many different resources to help you begin to understand dream symbolism. If you're uncertain which ones to use, ask Holy Spirit! He will guide you. Don't be lead by fear.

- The rule of first mention is a great place to start. This rule simply means the first time something shows up in the Bible, we can look at the Biblical context for understanding and definition. As mentioned earlier in the manual, in Genesis 3:1 it says, "The serpent was the most cunning of all wild animals that the Lord God made." From this first mention in the Bible, we can know that if a snake shows up in our dream, the Lord may be revealing a plan or scheme of the enemy of deception in our lives.

- Sometimes something illogical or unusual will happen in your dream. This can indicate a significant detail.

As an example of this last point, I had a dream several years ago where I was in an outdoor setting during the daytime. It was grey-scale and I was kind of down in my emotions. Suddenly, a flock of owls flew over my head. There were about five to seven of them and they were brown with white spots and speckles. In the dream, I thought to myself, "This is significant." The dream ended.

Once I set out to interpret the dream, I realized it broke a lot of interpretation "rules." Remember, we don't always want to rely on interpretation formulas. We want to ask the Holy Spirit. A few rules it broke: while this dream was muted in color, I knew it was from God; owls don't fly in flocks, they are typically loners; and owls usually only come out at night. What's so amazing is that I didn't have to wait to wake up to realize the flock of owls was significant! I told myself in the dream to pay attention to this detail.

After I woke, up I researched what a flock of owls is called. I discovered it's called a "parliament." For many years, I had longed for a healthy prophetic community and, perhaps, even to develop one. Sometimes, prophetic people have been loners, for one reason or another. In this dream, God was showing me that my heart's desire was being answered. A part of God's government being established in the earth is through healthy prophetic voices, in community with one another (for support and accountability), who will accurately convey His heart of love and declare Kingdom solutions into this world's problems.

Developing Your Dictionary through Your Native Language with God

As I've said throughout this manual, God loves to speak your language. As you begin to connect dots about the languages that are native to you, you'll gain a greater insight into what God's saying to you through your dream life. Below are some of my native symbols with God in dreams.

- Church – my mountain/call

- Husband – Jesus

- Sister – Holy Spirit or new creation me

- Cities – warfare

- Ears – spiritual hearing

- A watch – a change of season

- Classic trucks – ministry that's dear to my heart (I love classic trucks!)

Once you start to get a handle on symbolism and build your dictionary with the Lord, you'll begin to more instinctively know what your dreams mean.

One word of caution: no prophetic word or prophetic dream will ever take the place of Scripture. The Bible is the infallible Word of God, which means that there is no error in it whatsoever. Prophetic words are filtered through human flesh and dreams can be very ambiguous. It is tempting to base life direction on a prophetic word or dream. However, the Bible is the ultimate source we want to go to as we're making big life decisions. Additionally, wise counsel can help us discern direction and see things we may be blind to, due to zeal or offense, for instance. The Bible says that in the multitude of counselors there's safety (Proverbs 11:14). If you aren't sure what to do with a dream you receive, go to the Word, ask Holy Spirit, and talk with people in your community of trusted friends.

I had a dream in a season where I was desperately seeking God for direction. There is no doubt this dream came from God's heart. It was so full of life, excitement, peace, and the most gorgeous colors! I got the impression He was with me no matter the decision I made. However, in the natural, when I processed my decision based on the dream, I realized the timing was off. If I had decided to proceed with this big life decision that the dream blessed, it would have caused confusion and hurt to the precious people around me. Knowing that God is not the author of confusion (1 Corinthians 14:33), I chose to not proceed at the time. I decided to make my decision based on the Word, not a prophetic dream. This is a great way to make any decision in life. The Word of God has all the answers you need and you have the Holy Spirit with you always to breathe life on the path He'd like you to take.

Reflection

1. Why is it important to develop your own native language with the Lord? _____

_____

2. What are some important questions to ask about a dream when you set out to interpret it?

_____

3. Why does God often speak in symbols and metaphor? _____

_____

4. Why is it important to not rely on an interpretation formula? _____

_____

5. Why is it important to not rely on other people to interpret our dreams? _____

_____

Activation

Activation #1

Broaden your understanding of interpretation by answering these questions from what you learned in this chapter.

Dream Interpretation	
In the Bible, Joseph says interpretation belongs to…	
Most dreams are about…	
One of the biggest keys to interpreting a dream is asking…	
If a dream is full of color it may be…	
If a dream is grey or has muted color it may be…	
If a dream is dark it may be…	
Why is it good to write down or record the dream as soon as possible?	
Often if God shows you a concern about someone else it is an invitation to…	
If God shows up in a dream it will often be as…	

Activation #2

As with visions, dreams often have a lot of symbolism and metaphor. Continue to build your dictionary and define the following symbols. Use resources you feel comfortable with and ask the Holy Spirit! He may give you a new definition.

Kitchen	A mountain
A watch	Jewels/gems
Storms	Front lawn
Dove	The number 2
The number 3	The color red
A rainbow	A courtroom
A church	A bank
A turtle	Stars
Coins	A helicopter or plane

Activation #3

Take a shot at interpreting one of my dreams. I'd love to hear your thoughts! Please see my contact information at the end of this manual and email me your interpretation.

I had a most amazing dream last night. I was outside in an open grassy area with a small group of people. Suddenly, all these instruments came out of the sky and began to fly around us. All of the instruments had wings. It was amazing and awe-inspiring. Most of the instruments were trumpets, but one was a keyboard and that really caught my attention. Finally, the instruments landed. I told one of the girls there that I had had a dream about this very thing. I pulled out my journal and showed her in my journal where I had written the dream down and began to read to her from my

119

journal, "I had a most amazing dream last night. These instruments appeared in the sky and began to fly around us…" When I finished reading the dream to her, I looked around and began to take some pictures of the flying instruments, which were still landed on the ground but now without wings. There were some trumpets and a tuba (although I never saw it flying). The keyboard, however, wasn't there. The instruments formed a sculpture, like a steam punk thing. When I went to take a picture of the trumpets, they weren't there. For some reason, I think someone had taken them (although it didn't seem to be a negative thing). The dream ended.

Interpretation:

_____

_____

_____

_____

_____

_____

_____

The Honor of a King and Priest

"I will give you the keys of the kingdom of heaven, and whatever you bind on earth is already bound in heaven, and whatever you loose on earth is already loosed in heaven."
Matthew 16:19

God is bringing a new paradigm to the Body of Christ on intercession. It's really a revelation of what's always been there, but a paradigm shift, nonetheless. This new understanding is a forerunner to the sons and daughters of God being revealed in the earth and conquering every mountain for the Kingdom, with the authority Jesus bought back on the cross. You have authority. You have authority, in Jesus' Name, and a powerful partnership with the Holy Spirit to command any and every environment that doesn't reflect all the beauty of heaven to come into alignment and be changed. This is the power of intercession.

Intercession has long had a stigma as one of the least-desired posts in the Kingdom. When we say "intercession," sometimes we think of praying unceasingly, perhaps travailing, for hours. Who wants to do that? At least, it sure doesn't sound appealing. No matter the stigma, some people have dedicated their lives to intercession. I am most grateful for all the intercessors who have committed their lives in prayer to the Lord. It's these powerful, self-less saints who have furthered the Kingdom of God in the earth through their dedication to prayer and intercession when we, the majority of the Body, have been too preoccupied to be bothered with it.

When I address intercession in the Body of Christ, I am interested in dismantling a way of thinking. This way of thinking, or paradigm, has long relegated intercession to a lesser position within the Church. While we are grateful for the work of intercessors, often we don't fully understand the role, we certainly don't want to become one, and try at all costs to avoid it like the plague.

I hope you're still tracking with me.

Intercession, as with communion, tithing, or anything in the Body of Christ that is often misunderstood or shrouded in mystery, has tremendous value in the Kingdom. This is precisely why the enemy doesn't want us to grasp the full reality of it. As long as it has a shred of undesirability or confusion the enemy knows that we as a Body won't fully step into the power of intercession.

Intercession is not a gift. At least, intercession is not a gift in that it is not listed as one of the nine gifts of the Spirit in 1 Corinthians 12. Intercession is a function of every believer. We are *all* intercessors. Jesus, in fact, is an intercessor. He lives in us and lives to make intercession for us (Hebrews 7:25). Therefore, intercession is the privilege and responsibility of every disciple of Christ.

With all this being said, I do believe some people have a special grace and call to intercession. But I don't believe that only certain people are called to intercede, by the commonly-held understanding of what an "intercessor" is. We are all called to intercede. Just as with prophecy. We aren't all called as prophets, but the Bible says we can all prophesy!

Activation

As we go through this chapter, I'd like to you activate you at the beginning. Think of someone you know who doesn't know Jesus, someone who is addicted to drugs (prescription or illicit), or someone who isn't walking in the fullness of their destiny. Think about how you would apply what you learn to their situation as this chapter unfolds.

What Intercession Is Not

Before we discuss what intercession is, let's discover what intercession is not:

1. Tedious.

Intercession isn't a chore. Intercession isn't holing yourself up in a room and praying in the fetal position for hours (although if the Spirit of travail falls on you, that could certainly happen). Intercession can be done as you're walking through your local grocery store. The enemy wants us to think that intercession is the most boring task a believer could do because he knows there is so much power in it. Intercession is actually exhilarating. It's incredibly exciting to meet with the Lord and have Him direct us in prayer for a country, individual, or people group and be a catalyst for change in the earth. Intercessors are change agents. Although I may never know the entirety of the fruit of intercession until I get to heaven, often the process of intercession in partnering with the Holy Spirit brings incredible reward in knowing I'm following His lead to bring heaven to earth.

2. A lot of work or intense warfare.

Intercession is not synonymous with shouting, yelling, or screaming in tongues. Did you know you can bind and loose quietly or even silently? Did you know you can intercede with a joyful heart? There is a quietness that comes with Christ-like confidence. Of course, travail can happen as the Spirit leads. Romans 8:26 says, "In the same way the Spirit also joins to help in our weakness, because we do not know what to pray for as we should, but the Spirit Himself intercedes for us with unspoken groanings." It's interesting to note that the word *pray* here means *believing prayer* in the Greek. So, when we don't have the faith or strength to believe for a situation, the Holy Spirit comes alongside with *His* faith and intercedes for us. How's that for a Paraclete?[88] I think what we have done as a church, however, is defined intercession as labor, referencing this verse, and created a doctrine for intercessory travail. Now, if the Holy Spirit prompts you to travail, follow His lead. It's good, however, to consider your surroundings. My experience is that when I intercede as I'm walking through a mall, for instance, interceding quietly is usually more appropriate than yelling and groaning. Constant travail in intercession is restrictive.

3. Confusing or a mystery.

While intercession is not prayer, per se, it's also not confusing or mysterious. One of its functions is simply binding and loosing. We'll break down this aspect of intercession shortly.

4. Limited to a certain group of believers.

As mentioned in the introduction to this chapter, intercession is not always a call or gift. Intercession is the honor and responsibility of every believer.

5. Self-directed.

We can set out to meet the Lord to intercede, certainly. Especially when our hearts are moved with compassion. But it's my experience that intercession is usually a response to God's heart on a matter, whether that be an individual, people group, or nation. In other words, it's the Holy Spirit moving in intercession and we respond. You might be saying, "Wait, I thought you said you intercede when you're in the mall. How does the Spirit lead there?" For me, as I'm strolling the mall, I will sense God's heart for someone and intercede according to what I'm discerning. That conversation with God (in my heart or quietly, mind you) often looks like, "God, I see the depression or bondage in their life. I release your Holy Spirit to encounter them, minister to them, and set them free, in the Name of Jesus." My prayer is a response to His directing.

6. A list of prayer requests.

Intercession is not a prayer list. Intercession is a response to the Spirit on any given matter and an act to be carried out. We'll review different kinds of prayer in this chapter.

7. Anything negative you can think of.

Fill in the blank for yourself. What ideas, definitions, or stereotypes pop into your head when you hear the word "intercessor?" If any of those are negative, I would encourage you to invite the Lord to give you a paradigm shift on the matter.

Different Kinds of Biblical Prayer

Let's now look at how the Bible, in several places in the New Testament, defines different kinds prayer:

1. Agreeing Prayer

Matthew 18:19 says, "Again, I assure you: If two of you on earth agree about any matter that you pray for, it will be done for you by My Father in heaven." I like this kind of prayer a lot because it demonstrates the power of agreement. The Greek word *symphōneō*[89] here is where we get the word *symphony*. When we as believers are in one accord about a Kingdom solution or earthly matter, it's a beautiful symphony to God's ears!

2. Petition/Supplication

Philippians 4:6 says, "Do not be anxious about anything, but in every situation, by prayer and petition, with thanksgiving, present your requests to God." (NIV) These are petitions, coupled with a prayer to God, involving requests and needs that we entreat or ask of Him. It's the Greek word *deēsis*.[90] When there is a matter that concerns us and we invite God to help in that matter, it's defined by the Bible as a prayer of petition.

3. Believing Prayer

Luke 6:12 says, "Now it came to pass in those days that He went out to the mountain to pray, and continued all night in prayer to God." (NKJV) This word prayer, *proseuchomai*, literally translates, "a prayer addressed to God."[91] This is the same word used in Mark 11:24, "Therefore I say to you, whatever things you ask when you pray, believe that you receive them, and you will have them," and, interestingly, a form of this word is used in Matthew 17:21, "However, this kind does not go out except by prayer and fasting," (NKJV) We can, thus, define this as a prayer mixed with faith.

4. Thanksgiving

1 Timothy 2:1-2 really encapsulates a lot of different prayers. Paul covered all his bases. "First of all, then, I urge that petitions, prayers, intercessions, and thanksgivings be made for everyone, for kings and all those who are in authority, so that we may lead a tranquil and quiet life in all godliness and dignity." Colossians 4:2 says, "Devote yourselves to prayer; stay alert in it with thanksgiving." The specific prayer of thanksgiving, *eucharistia*, is a communication with God of gratefulness.[92]

5. Heart Prayer

James 5:16 says, "Therefore, confess your sins to one another and pray for one another, so that you may be healed. The urgent request of a righteous person is very powerful in its effect." 3 John 2 says, "Beloved, I pray that you may prosper in all things and be in health, just as your soul prospers." (NKJV) This word *euchomai* means a prayer or heart wish to God.[93]

Read through the above list again. Notice that none of these words are defined by or synonymous with intercession.

So, What is Intercession?[94]

Woo!!! This is where it gets exciting! You might be asking, "If intercession is not prayer, what is it?" I'm glad you asked!

There are many facets to intercession, which we will break down in this chapter. As you read through them, invite the Holy Spirit to give you revelation from His heart on the importance of this powerful Kingdom honor!

1. Intercession is more of an action than a prayer.

Think of the difference between asking God to set someone free and actually going to the jail cell and opening the door. One is a request and the other is an action. While we don't literally set someone free (that's the Holy Spirit's job), we are exercising the authority that Jesus bought back by His blood to declare someone free, loose them from bondages, and bind up the spirits at work in their lives.

2. Intercession is the privilege of a king.

King Jesus died on the cross to get all authority back that the enemy deceived Adam and Eve into giving away. When all authority was returned to Him, by His shed blood and death, Jesus gave *us* those keys of authority to the Kingdom, so that whatever we bind on earth will be bound and whatever we loose on earth will be loosed. Once sinners, the Bible says that we are now not only new creations, but we are also kings and priests (see 1 Peter 1:9 and Revelation 1:6). As kings, a function of our role is to exercise our delegated authority in the earth to bind and loose, as representatives of heaven.

3. Intercession is the honor of a priest.

A priestly role is one of intimacy. The more we spend time with Jesus, the more intimate we get with Him. The more intimate we get with Him, the more we get to know His heart on any matter and desire to be His ministers on the earth. I'm not talking about a position in the church. I'm talking about a position of the heart. Ministering to God is one of the greatest honors we have on this earth. Ministering to Him can look like worshipping Him and blessing Him for who He is as the kind and loving, yet uncreated One. It might look like giving Him counsel on a matter (see Genesis 18:16-33).

This honor can also look like processing with Him. The Bible tells us to mourn with those who mourn. I've heard people say that God is always happy. This is absolutely true as it relates to us as His kids. He always has a smile in His heart towards us. But have you ever thought about how He feels when a young child gets violated? His heart grieves. Have you ever thought about who mourns with God or comforts *Him*? You might think this contradicts what I've stated above about interceding from a heart of joy. But the Bible is full of tensions. The Word says there is a time and season for everything. It would be most inappropriate to minister to a family, telling them to be joyful, when they've just lost a child to some horrible disease or car accident. Mourning with God is a response to His heart when He shows us tragedies in the earth. This is completely different than ministering from a position of defeat or depression. It's an act of compassion.

The priestly function is also ministering on behalf of people. Nations, cities, people groups, and individuals are hanging in the balance. Our priestly role is to minister to God on behalf of them, to advocate for them; for freedom, peace, restoration, and redemption. God wants to release mercy and grace. We can apply all the benefits of the cross through our priestly role of intercession.

4. Intercession births what the prophetic impregnates.

Intercession is as vitally important to the Body of Christ as prophecy. The prophetic impregnates the earth or the hearer with the promises of God and intercession is what often births those promises. Amos 3:7 says, "Indeed, the Lord God does nothing without revealing His counsel to His servants the prophets." When the time comes for a declared word to be accomplished, God begins to alert the Body or individuals to intercede for the promise. Those who discern and make themselves available act like midwives to partner with the Spirit in birthing the very thing God wants to accomplish in the earth. It's been my experience that if you find a prophet who's really cultivated an intimacy with God, coupled with humility, you'll often find in that same person a dedicated intercessor. It's good to note that God's *kairos*,[95] or strategic, timing is much different than natural, or *kronos*,[96] timing. God has designated times and seasons in the Spirit to accomplish His purposes. We discern these birthing times and seasons in the Spirit.

5. Intercession is like building a bridge from heaven to earth.

Isaiah 59:16 says, "The Lord saw that there was no justice, and He was offended. He saw that there was no man—He was amazed that there was no one interceding." God cares deeply about justice. And He is very passionate about us partnering with Him to release justice into any and every circumstance needing it. The word intercede in this passage is the Hebrew word *paga*, which can mean a go-between.[97] Picture yourself holding God's hand and the hand of the person you know who is suicidal. You are the bridge between the two, advocating on their behalf, as the Holy Spirit prompts and leads, and being a conduit for the Holy Spirit to minister God's heart to them. You are building a bridge between their earthly circumstance and heaven's solutions. God is looking for partners who will be available to work with Him to change earth to look like heaven. He's looking for Kingdom bridge builders.

6. Intercession is giving a voice to the voiceless.

Intercession is like a work of advocacy. Romans 8:26 gives us insight into how the Holy Spirit functions for *us* when we don't know how to pray. He is the One who speaks on our behalf when we are burdened or can't find the right words to utter. Similarly, when we intercede on behalf of someone to break bondages in their life, for instance, we are praying the prayer they are either too blind or too bound to pray. Think of a pimp or drug dealer. We can minister to God on their behalf, declaring His mercy through Jesus' shed blood, and release (loose) encounters with His love.

7. Intercession is what Jesus does.

Hebrews 7:25 says that Jesus always lives to intercede for us. Jesus died on the cross so we could be reconciled to the Father and grafted into His family. After His resurrection and ascension, Jesus took His place at the right hand of God and now lives to make intercession for us! Isn't that amazing? He now intercedes so that we might live in the fullness of what He purchased on the cross. How's that for self-sacrifice? He lived on the earth to die for us and now He lives in heaven to intercede for us. Once we invited Jesus into our hearts, He moved in. If, then, Jesus lives in us, we are intercessors because He is an intercessor.

Biblical Definition of Intercession

In the Hebrew, the word "intercession" is often the word *paga* which can be defined as the following:

To encounter, to meet, to strike a boundary, to lay upon, to come (betwixt), or to hit the mark.[98]

In the Greek, the word "intercession" is *enteuxis,* which is defined as the following:

A falling in with, a meeting with, a coming together, or converse or for any other cause.[99]

From these two different languages, we can see that intercession is an action in which we set up an appointment, a meeting, for a person or any situation with the Spirit of God. Setting up the encounter is the priestly function of intercession.

I have a friend whose sister was bound by all sorts of things: drugs, sexual bondage, fear, anxiety, etc. She had a stroke at the age of about 25. I would often find myself interceding for her. What I mean by this is that my heart would often turn towards her as I felt the Holy Spirit prompting me. One day, I was playing electric bass to a certain worship song and began to see in the Spirit. As I played and sang, I realized I was singing the words directly to her as if I was the Lord: "No matter who you are, no matter where you run, no matter what you do, what you're going through...everyone's someone."[100] Over and over I would sing to her and minister God's heart. I would release in the Spirit the truth that she had value and worth. I did this for about a half hour or more. As I interceded, I could see the Holy Spirit spinning around her like a translucent light. He would spin around her with such speed, light, and love. I knew that He was ministering to her. My partnering with Him, in response to His heart, set up the encounter.

Intercession can also mean to "strike a boundary." We have authority as Jesus' delegates to draw boundaries in the spirit realm. The Holy Spirit may prompt us to draw a line in the spirit and declare that the enemy will no longer overstep bounds in a person's life or situation. Or we can be proactive in preparing an environment. We may not sense anything negative but feel prompted to strike a boundary in a corporate setting. This is often pre-emptive in nature. Setting up a boundary in the spirit can be as simple as declaring, "In the Name of Jesus, nothing is allowed in this room that doesn't exist in God's world. No fear, anger, shame, or confusion." This can be done very calmly and peacefully. Exercising authority over the demonic realm is a kingly function of intercession.

Binding and Loosing

We each have a role to play in the affairs of God on earth. While God doesn't really need us to use our gifts to accomplish anything for Him, He delights in having his sons and daughters work *with* Him to release heaven into the world's problems. God's heart is that we would fully grasp all that Jesus purchased on the cross (mercy and grace, love, joy, peace, freedom from bondage and sin, etc.) and rise up as kings and priests to change the world. Side note, when I say rise up, I don't mean getting puffed up. Pride is not the same thing as confidence. We can be confident, knowing who we are in Christ, and approach every situation with a heart of humility.

As we've seen, intercession has a kingly and priestly function. The enemy doesn't want us to connect the dots on this (or anything of Kingdom significance). As kings and priests, we have the privilege and responsibility of extending God's government in the earth through Christ's delegated authority. He wants us to command things that are out of alignment with what Jesus paid for on the cross to realign with heaven. He also invites us minister to His heart on behalf of the hurting world. The common thread of a priest and king is intercession.

Jesus is the original Prophet, Priest and King. We, too, are prophetic priests and kings. Revelation 1:5b-6 says, "Unto him (Jesus) that loved us, and washed us from our sins in his own blood, and hath made us kings and priests unto God and his Father; to him be glory and dominion for ever and ever. Amen (AKJV, parenthesis added)." Jesus saved us and set us free to change the world, so that those bound can also experience freedom and, in turn, change the world. It's a domino effect. In Matthew 28:18 Jesus says, "All authority has been given to Me in heaven and on earth." He got back all authority and is looking for people to exercise it.

In Matthew 16:19 He also says that He has given us the keys to the Kingdom of heaven, "...and whatever you bind on earth is already bound in heaven, and whatever you loose on earth is already loosed in heaven." Not only have we been given the keys of authority, but as we use those keys we find circumstances already bound and loosed in heaven. It's already done. When Jesus said "it is finished," He meant it. He is simply looking for family on the earth who will believe everything the Word says and enforce it!

The word "keys" in this passage means two things in the Greek:

> A literal key: Since the keeper of the keys has the power to open and to shut.
> A metaphoric term to represent power and authority of various kinds.[101]

Jesus is the Key Master and He's given keys to us as His delegated authority on the earth to open and shut, loose and bind (see Isaiah 22:22; Revelation 3:7). Think about that for a moment. The same God Who created the universe has chosen *us* to be His delegates on earth! We're talking about a major honor here. God has chosen YOU to change the world. This isn't a marketing tagline or clever slogan. This is what God has set up to transform this earth!

Mark 13:34 says, "It is like a man on a journey, who left his house, gave authority to his slaves, gave each one his work, and commanded the doorkeeper to be alert." God delegated His authority to us not only to demonstrate for other people what the Kingdom of heaven is like, but to establish His Kingdom on earth, through the Name of Jesus. He's given each one of us a purpose and call, as part of His master plan. And He's given each one of us authority to carry out our part of that plan.

As we discussed earlier in the manual, Isaiah 9:7 says, "Of the increase of His government and peace there will be no end..." (NKJV) This means that wherever you go, the Kingdom goes. Wherever you go peace goes, to change earth to look more and more like heaven's government. So, if we put two and two together, we are God's agents on earth to help in the increase of His heavenly government, His rule and dominion, via the delegated authority Jesus gave us, through the vehicle of peace.

God has given us each a customized purpose on this planet. Whatever spheres of influence we're in, we're called to bring God's government of peace to it. If you walk into an angry, tense atmosphere, bind up anger and release peace. If you walk into a room full of fear, bind it up and release God's perfect love.

Job 22:28 says, "You will also declare a thing, and it will be established for you." (NKJV) When we make declarations that God is making, when we say what He's saying, those decrees are sure to be established! God wants us to work with Him to loose Godly decrees and bind up ungodly decrees. If it doesn't belong in heaven, it's gotta be bound here on the earth! If it's heaven's reality but not present here, we get to loose it in the earth. This is how we can have a demonized person come up to us and we calmly say, "I command torment to leave and peace to fill you, in Jesus' Name," without yelling or getting fearful. We have a positional authority in Christ and permission to make decrees on His behalf. He's given us His signet ring.

Prophetic Intercession

You may have heard of the term "prophetic intercession." There is a bit of a distinction between prophetic intercession and intercession, although they essentially accomplish the same thing. The difference between the two types of intercession is that with prophetic intercession God will shows us what He wants to do, prophetically speaking, and we declare it and agree. Like the example I used on page 65 in the chapter on prophecy, this can happen proactively to partner with Him in what He wants to do in a church service, for instance. Often, before we go into an environment, we can ask God what's on His heart and then partner with Him to release (loose) what He shows us or bind up what is not of Him, as He leads. It is amazing to watch these things play out in the natural. It is incredibly encouraging and faith-building.

With intercession, on the other hand, the Holy Spirit may prompt us at any time, even when we aren't actively seeking Him for a specific environment or situation. In a devotional time or during a worship service, for instance, the Holy Spirit may prompt us to intercede for something. We may have no idea what "it" is, we just know that He's drawing us in to partner with Him to enforce a spiritual victory. We then pray it through until we have a release. This facet of intercession requires a little more faith and trust. We may never know until we get to heaven what we're partnering with God in binding or loosing, bridge-building or birthing, but we can know that the Holy Spirit is inviting us to partner with Him for outcomes of incredible eternal significance.

Examples of Different Kinds of Intercession

- Sometimes during worship, I will stand in the place of the person I know who is on drugs or in some type of bondage and sing the worship song *as if I'm them*. I am singing what they can't sing. They don't know how to pray or ask for help because they're in bondage, so I sing it for them as an act of intercession.

- When I was in the world, there were many nights that I wouldn't come home. My parents often didn't know what to do but pray. On one particular night, my mom said that the Spirit woke her up and prompted her to intercede. In fact, there was nothing she could say but "the blood of Jesus" for about an hour. She said that night I came home at about three in the morning. When I walked in, I had a deer-in-headlights look on my face. She said I then explained that I was downtown at a bar and when I went to get a drink, the bartender said, "Honey, you have got to go home. You have blood all over you." In the natural, I didn't have blood on me but, to this day, I don't know if the Lord allowed the bartender to see the blood of Jesus in the spirit or if she was an angel. What I do know is that this act of intercession saved me from who-knows-what and brought me home.

- I lead a ministry trip to England in 2013 to be part of a regional conference. One night, during the ministry time, a mother approached me, distraught about her young adult son. She said that he was on drugs and hadn't been home in weeks. She told me she feared the worst. I released my testimony of how God saved my life from drug abuse and days away from home, which increased her faith and released grace (see Revelation 19:10). I then, in the Name of Jesus, spoke to her son's spirit, since there is no time or distance in the spirit realm, and I blessed him. I told him he was so loved and had great value and worth and that God had an amazing destiny for him. The next night, he came to the meeting! He told his mom he "didn't know why," but *felt* he had to be there. Note: Although he was in a lifestyle of drug abuse and away from home, he discerned by his spirit that the Spirit of God was calling him home.

- One day I was in a local superstore and within the span of about one minute, I encountered three different dads, each with kids in their carts. All three of them were emotionally engaged, warm, and loving towards their children. I thought, "That is unusual. You don't see that often." This especially got my attention because it was all within the timeframe of about a minute. I knew immediately, prophetically speaking, that the Lord wanted me to declare Malachi 4:6, "And He will turn the hearts of the fathers to their children and the hearts of the children to their fathers." I then acknowledged that this was God's heart and interceded that He would do it on a mass scale in the earth! Part of restoring the Kingdom on earth is restoring families. What this prayer looked like for me was, "God I see that You want to do this in the earth and I agree. God, You are turning the hearts of fathers to their children and children to their fathers. Family was your idea, God, and I bless this great idea. I partner with You in this."

The Heart of Intercession

As with any language of the Spirit, God is inviting us to dialogue with Him. As we make ourselves available and discern when He's prompting us, He begins to speak to us about what is on His heart.

Our surrender to God is not an act of abasement or a groveling, and it's not one where we lose our personality. Our surrender to Him is an act of humility and honor. And it's in this place, ironically, that we discover our true selves. We say with our words, actions, and hearts, "Here's my life, Lord, I lay it down. How can I join You in what You're doing today?"

Isaiah 53:10 says that it pleased God to crush Christ on the cross. Not so you and I can walk around saying "I am nothing." Our false humility re-crucifies Him. It pleased God to crush Christ on the cross so that through Him we could be His sons and daughters, His priests and kings, extending His Kingdom on earth. It pleased God to crush Christ so that we could be royalty, extending the authority of Dad in the earth. It pleased Him to crush Jesus because He knew the great return on the investment He was making.

Now, through Christ, we have been given the ministry of reconciliation. We have been given the ministry of peace. We have been given the ministry of calling what is not as though it is![102]

It pleased God to crush Christ on the cross so that all the harm and havoc, the killing and destroying that the enemy intended for each of one of us throughout the timeline of history, would be turned on satan's head. Through Christ's heart of humility, He said, "Take this cup from me, Dad. I don't want to do this. However, I surrender My will for Yours."

He surrendered His will and, ultimately, His life that there would be co-heirs on this planet who would go low in humility, just like He did, to change the world. The exact opposite spirit, the spirit of pride, that drove satan out of God's presence and caused him to be shot like lightning out of heaven.[103] God is looking for self-less daughters and sons who will surrender their lives in humility and say, "Papa, not my will but Yours…"

It's in this place of surrender, this place of crushing, that the anointing is cultivated in you and me. It's in this sweet place of humility that the anointing of God can break yokes of bondage. God wants to empower us to reconcile hurting people to Christ, people who don't know that they've already been reconciled to Him! His heart is that we would all eat at the banqueting table together. He has set this feasting table for us in the presence of the enemy who chose pride and selfishness over God's presence. God can't wait for all His kids to come back home and celebrate with Him.

It was always God's plan for us to partner with Him here on earth. He put us here to cultivate and manage it so it looks like heaven. He's given us the keys to the Kingdom!

Reflection

1. What misconceptions have you had about intercession? _____

_____

_____

2. How do you look at intercession differently after reading this chapter? _____

_____

_____

3. In what ways will you live as a king and priest going forward? _____

_____

_____

4. In what ways do you feel God has called you, uniquely, to extend His Kingdom in earth?

_____

_____

Activation

Activation #1

Put on worship music. Write down three to five things that make you incredibly angry, mad, or passionate regarding justice issues in this world. Ask the Holy Spirit for keys in partnering with Him in intercession for breakthrough in these areas.

Activation #2

Find an old key (house key, car key, etc.) and then ask God to show you a specific circumstance or situation in your personal life that needs breakthrough. Ask Him to give you a key to binding up or loosing with the authority He's given you. Use the key as a prompter for faith and reminder to make declarations.

Activation #3

Psalm 2:8 says to ask of God and He will give us the nations. Search out an image of a world map, print it, and ask the Holy Spirit which nation or nations He would like to share His heart about. Begin dialoguing with Him on it. Intercede as He leads.

Spiritual Tidbits

"Drink deeply..." (NKJV)
Song of Songs 5:1

We will never reach the end of discovering God. Just when we feel we've experienced Him in fullness, He invites us to delight in another dimension of His nature. Everything we experience in the Spirit, all the gifts, spiritual experiences and supernatural encounters, are meant to continually point us back to Him. These spiritual experiences are never meant to be an end unto themselves. It may seem like splitting hairs but we can often get sidetracked in pursuing the things of God and lose connection with God Himself. Conversely, as we press in to pursue Him more, we find that there is layer upon layer, revelation upon revelation that He joyously pours out in a place of intimacy.

We will most likely never encounter true intimacy with Him, however, until and unless we intentionally create that sacred place for ourselves. I can read about other's encounters with His presence all day long, but until I position my heart to connect with Him myself, it will always remain someone else's revelation and someone else's experience.

God longs to spend time with you. His heart aches at the thought of being the closest and most intimate person to you. He is overcome with joy when He realizes that He becomes priority in our lives and then it's almost as if He has to restrain everything within Him to try and hold back the myriad of blessings He has for us. He's like a giddy Dad at Christmas who wants to shower His children with everything He has but His wisdom wins out over excitement, knowing that some blessings are best reserved for a time of our demonstrated maturity.

Cultivating intimacy is not difficult. It's simply turning your heart towards Him and experiencing His goodness. He wants you to find Him! Ask God to show you *how* to meet with Him, *how* to encounter Him, *how* to experience Him. Turn your thoughts towards Him. Drink in Love. He is the King of kings and Lord of lords, yes. But He is also a gentle Shepherd. He is the only One who will love you the way that you need to be loved, even those unspoken and unarticulated heart needs.

This practice of intimacy is just that. It takes practice. We need to intentionally quiet our clamorous soul and begin the journey of developing relationship with God. Often our soul want to seek any and every satisfaction *but* Him, much to its own dismay. Yet, our spirit knows that our soul's voracious need for affection and belonging can only be satisfied in Jesus.

Set your heart on a pilgrimage.[104] Purpose to discover Him. He's a person and He longs for relationship just like you do. And then, ironically, once your soul gets a taste of the beauty of God, it begins to reject anything that falls short of His Presence.

Spiritual Tidbits

This chapter is filled with some spiritual odds and ends for you to peruse. Some of them may seem a bit random, but my heart is that they may challenge, inspire, or encourage you in your journey with God.

Know Yourself

In cultivating intimacy with God, it's good to know yourself. I am not a morning person. In fact, I pretty much loathe morning. I am a night owl. Always have been and always will be. This is important to know when I set out to meet with God. My prime time is about 2:00 p.m. in the afternoon. If I try to model my time with God after spiritual greats who have gone before me, those who rise at 4:00 a.m. to meet with God, I will be (and have been) very frustrated.

Additionally, my personality is one that likes brevity and spontaneity. When I spend time with God, often a short and sweet approach works for my busy life. I find, also, that I often like to change up when and where I meet with Him or bounce around in the Bible. Sometimes I chastise myself for the inability to stay in one place in the Word, but then I realize that it's often my personality or the Holy Spirit (or the Holy Spirit through my personality) and take the fun roller coaster ride through my devotion time.

What constraints do you have in meeting with God? If you're a busy mom, sometimes the best, and only, time you'll get is on the toilet for two minutes. However, you and I both know that within that time tiny hands (and paws) will be peeking out from under the door to try and vie for that precious time. Sometimes the constraints we have are mental. Are you trying to meet with God the way your parents or pastor does? Are you trying to kneel by your bed for hours with little to no results? You have to make your walk your own. It's the only way it will be fruitful and authentic.

You are a mobile Holy of Holies. You are a walking prayer closet. The Bible tells us to pray continuously and the only and best way to do that is throughout our day. If we only pray in our prayer closets there would be no one to take God's mandate to extend the Kingdom throughout the earth. God wants to shift our paradigm of what constant union looks like.

Now, there are definitely times to get alone with God. Jesus did this and He is our example. There are also times when God will draw us out of the comfort zones in which our personalities thrive. There was one season, in particular, when God denied me of what I thought was the greatest desire of my heart and invited me into, what I call, a priestly season. I would drop our son off at school in the morning in my pajamas and hurry home to meet with Him. I would make coffee, toast pumpkin chocolate chip bread, open the window to the rainy, dark day and get back in bed. I would study and pray and encounter Him for hours. Finally, I would realize it was time to get our son from school and beg God to stretch out time. It was the most incredible season of my life. I was convinced that I wanted to spend a cloistered life ministering to Him. It was in this season that He began to deposit within me what I would need for my call which, as it turns out, is more of a public ministry and a far cry from what I thought I so desperately wanted for my life at the start of the priestly season.

Seek God. Trust Him. Delight in Him and He will give you the desires of your heart. But sometimes He'll take away the position or call you think you want, rewire you, and give you the purpose for which you were created. You have to be courageous. Like I tell our students, Winnie the Pooh says it best, "Be brave little Piglet."[105] Be brave.

The Garden of Your Heart

Matthew 5:8 says that the pure in heart will see God. If we want to see God like Moses did and learn more about His world, purity of heart is a key to breakthrough. Moses demonstrated this through a heart of humility. What areas of our lives are filled with anger, gossip, offense, fear, or self-driven agenda? These things can be obstacles to our connection with God. No one can cure or preserve the condition of our hearts but us and the Holy Spirit. Keeping our hearts pure is a priority if we want to go deeper into His Presence.

Everything started in a garden. This was God's intention: union thriving in an atmosphere teeming with life and love. As you know, man was eventually kicked out of the garden due to some poor choices. It wasn't until Jesus that all was redeemed for mankind. In a garden, Jesus surrendered His will to the will of His Dad, knowing you and I would be the reward. He prayed in a garden, cried in a garden, and made the decision to redeem and restore humanity in a garden. Now, Jesus wants to meet with us in the garden of our heart! However, sometimes our hearts look a lot different from the place He wants to call home. It's our responsibility to maintain the soil, pull out weeds, and nurture our garden. The more our hearts look like heaven, the more we will experience Him.

The Hungry Will Be Filled

Much of what we move in, regarding our spiritual gifts and understanding the languages of the Spirit, lies in our anticipation and cultivation of those gifts. We must believe that He exists and that He's a rewarder of those who diligently seek Him (Hebrews 11:6). We must believe that the spiritual gifts are for everyone; nothing is off limits. As stated in this manual, if it's in the Bible, it's ours by legal access in Christ. We must believe that God is a kind Dad and that He gives good gifts.[106] Matthew 5:6 says that the hungry will be filled. If we hunger for the things of God, He will satisfy us and bless us in ways unimaginable! What are you hungering for?

Kronos vs. Kairos Timing

I remember one particular season of life I so desperately wanted to step more fully into destiny. I didn't know why God seemed to be relatively silent. I was incredibly frustrated about what seemed to be a delay. To be honest, I was a brat. After months of frustration and apologies for my childish, entitled behavior towards Him, I realized that the timing of my destiny didn't matter as much as my intimacy with Him. Pride was elevating my selfishness above His heart and my spirit's desire to commune with Him. I slowly (and did I mention slowly?) realized He was really all I needed. He held all the answers I wanted. And, in His timing, He would reveal next steps.

As mentioned earlier in this book, *kronos* time is like a timeclock. It is linear time by which we as humans live our lives. *Kairos* time is a different kind of time. It is a strategic, opportune, "fitting" time. God doesn't work according to our clock. He has much more advanced, purposeful times in which He conducts business.

In reflection of this season, I wrote this in my journal:

What if kronos time as we know it became inferior and nearly inconsequential in our approach to life with God? What if the whispers of His workings (signs, symbols, visions, impressions) were invitations, real, tangible invitations into His cosmic "timing?" Not linear, but vastly spacial and ubiquitous. What if our approach wasn't to seek a timeline but seek the Father of time Himself; an invitation to partner at a whole different level and dimension?

I realized that my spoiled, myopic view of life was greatly limiting me and my relationship with God. You see, our spirits often know instinctively what season we're in, but our flesh demands answers that are often out of season. Ecclesiastes 3:1 says that there is a time and season for everything. Like the sons of Issachar, we want to become astute in discerning the times and seasons God has appointed (1 Chronicles 12:32). Once we tell our flesh that it won't be leading, it ceases to be as noisy and demanding and we can be free to meet God where He's working in any season. It actually liberates us to occupy a wider space with a fresh Spirit paradigm. The Bible says that the flesh profits nothing and it's the Spirit that gives life (John 6:63). My heart is to constantly stay connected to the life-giving Spirit of God, no matter how counter-intuitive it may be, so that everything I do bears fruit for the Kingdom. Ask God with an expectancy about the season you're in.

Déjà Vu

In another season of life, my family was about to make a huge life change. My sister had come down to Bakersfield, CA, where we were living at the time, to help us pack and move up to Northern California, where I was going to start ministry school. She and I ran out to the store one night to get some supplies. As we were driving slowly through the parking lot, suddenly, I had the most vivid déjà vu I had ever experienced.

Instinctively and immediately I knew that my spirit had been to that exact place before. Remember, there is no time or distance in the Spirit. Job 33:15 says, "In a dream, in a vision of the night, when deep sleep falls upon men, while slumbering on their beds, then He opens the ears of men, and seals their instruction. In order to turn man from his deed, and conceal pride from man, He keeps back his soul from the pit, and his life from perishing by the sword." Our spirits are awake even when we sleep and can receive from God, interact with Him, and travel to the places He leads.

God spoke to my heart that night, through the phenomena of déjà vu, that I was smack dab in the middle of my destiny! I felt such a peace and confirmation that we, as a family, were stepping more fully into the place that He had prepared for us. It was an amazing experience and exhilarating feeling to know that God is always ahead and always preparing us. We simply have to make ourselves available, dare to believe new things, and listen for His whispers.

Your Spirit Knows

Have you ever started gravitating towards certain colors, images, pictures, or Scriptures? Ever wonder why you feel lead to do something but have no context or concrete reason as to why? As I mentioned earlier, this can be an indication that your spirit instinctively knows (discernment) what season you're in or is perceiving the season you're about to step into. Remember, pay attention to the things that get your attention!

There was a time when I loved the color blue. About 10 years later, I started to be drawn to the color red. Everything in my house started to shift towards this new color palette. In reflection, I began to realize that my heart for the prophetic (blue) started to move towards a desire to build and take action (red). I absolutely love revelation but I have a passion to take that revelation and help build the Kingdom on earth.

There was another time when I felt lead to listen to Gregorian chants. I had absolutely no clue why, I just felt a strong pull. This was a season of profound transition and rewiring. I felt such an internal struggle. At one point, I went to the Internet and found a chant by Benedictine monks. I listened to it continuously. Again, I had no concrete reason "why" except, perhaps, that my last name is Monk and I do love mystical experiences! Yet, the music *felt* wonderful and really "resonated" with me.

About a year later, I started reading a book called *The Physics of Heaven* by Judy Franklin and Ellyn Davis. I was shocked (but not really surprised) at what I read: "The term 'resonate' literally means to 'return to sound.' Music was used to 'tune' the body to its natural 'sound,' its natural resonant frequency. In Christian tradition, music has also been considered to have healing powers. Many of the great cathedrals in Europe were designed to be harmonic resonating chambers for sound and music to heal, amplify, and alter consciousness during worship and prayer. And Gregorian chants were based on the Solfeggio frequencies, special tones believed to have transformative power and impart spiritual blessings." [107]

I was amazed! God lead me to a style of music that would be very healing for me in a season of upheaval and uncertainty. A Biblical example of music having healing powers is when Saul asked David to play the harp. When David did, the tormenting spirits that were troubling Saul left. Now, I wasn't troubled demonically, but God knew that I was certainly off-kilter and needed to find a place of peace to help navigate the season I was in.

While There Is No Competition in the Kingdom...

There is no competition in the Kingdom of heaven. There is plenty of destiny to go around. There is no comparison or striving to be better than the next guy. The Kingdom is about unity and community. Competition and comparison are rooted in pride. However, while the Kingdom of heaven is not marked by rivalry, there is one thing God wants us to out-do each other in: love.

Seek and You Will Find...

A good indication of where we're at spiritually, what we're hungering for, or what we're seeking from God is to take a look at the prayers we're praying. This is a prayer I wrote in my journal in 2012:

"Teach me. Teach me how to go deeper in You. Teach me how to get lost in You. Teach me how to meditate. Teach me how to meditate on Your Word. Teach me how to abide in You. Teach me how to fully surrender. Teach me how to be unoffendable. Teach me how to hear Your voice more clearly. Teach me how to love You. Teach me how to learn. Teach me how to see the Kingdom. Teach me to follow You. Teach me how to follow You."

Matthew 7:7-8 says, "Keep asking, and it will be given to you. Keep searching, and you will find. Keep knocking, and the door will be opened to you. For everyone who asks receives, and the one who searches finds, and to the one who knocks, the door will be opened."

No Fear!

There was a time in my life when I was continually drawn to all-things-quantum. Now, let me preface this by saying that I have a degree in English. My mathematical expertise and extent goes as far as 2 +2 = 4. Beyond that, I need a calculator. While I'm fascinated with and appreciate the world of science, I wouldn't say that I have a great mental capacity to understand it, either. God will often invite us into things that go *way* beyond our ability to comprehend. This is the nature of revelation. Acts tells us that Jesus called unschooled, ordinary men. 1 Corinthians 1 shows us that God actually takes pleasure in choosing the foolish things of this world to confound the wise. Now, I'm not saying that I'm foolish, nor am I developing a doctrine for idiocy. There is a difference between stupidity and humility. God is looking for tender hearts to deposit profound revelation in which to wow the world.

During a season of invitation from God to learn about the quantum world, I started to get an increased amount of fear surrounding the topic. Thoughts like, "Be careful, this is New-Agey," or "You are opening yourself up to deceit. This stuff isn't in the Bible," would flood my mind. I started to get so scared of the topic that finally one day I cried out to God and said, "God! If this is You inviting me into learning about the quantum world, then You need to confirm it. Otherwise, I will walk away from this pursuit."

The next day, I went to get my hair done. As I was walking out of the salon, I turned and right in front of me was a car with the word "QUANTLM" on the license plate! I knew it was God!!! And I should have known that the broker of fear, the enemy, was trying to scare me off of an amazing journey of discovery lead by the Holy Spirit Himself.

There is to be no fear in our discovery process. Sometimes fear can be an indication that we are on the right track. Fear can intensify incredibly just before an immense breakthrough or revelation. Talk with God. Ask Him about what you're experiencing. Ask Him to confirm what He's inviting you into. If you still don't have clarity, talk with like-minded community who can pray and seek God with you. But, whatever you do, don't partner with fear.

Supernatural Healing

Although we've touched on it throughout this manual, supernatural healing could have its own chapter. In fact, entire books could be and have been written on this topic. Supernatural physical healing is one of the ways that God demonstrates His love for His kids. Can you imagine living with a disease, physical impairment, or illness for years and then suddenly being supernaturally healed? Think of the amazement, awe, and wonder it would inspire within your heart.

For me, the argument of whether God still heals today is silly at best, unbiblical at worst. To say that God doesn't heal doesn't line up with His nature. Besides, why in the world would I want to serve a God who is either incapable or refuses to move in supernatural power to remedy the natural world of its problems? I believe in a God who is the greatest King to have ever walked this planet, a King who served with a heart of love. This same King still serves and heals today, and He often does so through you and me.

When God extends love through the language of healing to His children, no translation is needed. Remember the woman with the issue of blood? She bled continually for 12 years. Think about that for a moment. Think about the inconvenience, frustration, hopelessness, and humiliation it would breed within a person. The instant she was healed, she experienced the overwhelming love of God. Throughout the New Testament Jesus only did what He saw His Father doing and His Father was always working to make crooked places straight, revealing destiny to those without hope, and healing people - spirit, soul, and body. It's no different today.

I would encourage you to get your hands on the many great books and resources out there on the topic of supernatural healing. Pastor Bill Johnson has been a catalyst and hero of mine in this area.

The Languages of the Spirit Can Often Change

Have you ever wondered why God has stopped talking? This is a bit of a trick question, because God is always communicating with us. It just may not be, however, on the topic we want to discuss. He's always communicating because He longs to connect with us.

Sometimes the reason God "isn't talking" is because He's changing up the *way* He's talking. It may be because He wants us to grow in our understanding of Him and His world. It can be because we are getting too comfortable in our relationship with Him. Or it could be that He's opening up a new realm of connection with Him. God is always looking for ways to draw us in.

I had a dream one night that there was a little dove (Holy Spirit) on a branch of a tree that was outside of our house in the back yard. As I was sitting on our bench under the tree, I looked above me and the little bird was chirping away. I could tell he was trying to communicate with me. Yet, as he was "talking," I couldn't understand him. In the dream, I said to him, "I know you're talking to me but I don't know what you're saying." When I woke up, I knew God was changing up the way

He was communicating with me. My heart was then set in a position of expectancy to meet and hear from Him in a new way.

Man Does Not Live on Bread Alone

There is no life apart from the Word. That is a bold statement but a true one nonetheless. We can have no meaningful life apart from Jesus because He is the Word. The problem for many of us is either finding a passion to get into the Bible or knowing where to start.

A few pointers for getting into the Word of God:

- Ask God for a hunger to read the Bible. Years ago, I was working at a company and would go out into my car to pray and read the Word at lunch time. I would frequently get sleepy or fall asleep. I finally prayed, "God! Your Word is boring. I'm so sorry, but it makes me fall asleep. I don't connect to it at all. Please give me a hunger to get into your Word, because I know it's important." Guess what!? He did. He deposited a supernatural hunger within me to read the Bible.

- Find a Bible translation that works for you. King James Version? For me, no thank you. Who talks like that today? I have a degree in English literature and hate Shakespeare (what English major ever hated Shakespeare? Me.). Reading the Word can be hard enough without having to overcome a language barrier. Find a translation that makes understanding and applying the Word easy. Audio Bibles are also awesome if you drive or travel a lot.

- Remember that when you are reading the Bible, you are getting to know a Person. John 1:1 says, "In the beginning was the Word and the Word was with God and the Word was God." Revelation 19:13 says that Jesus wears "a robe stained with blood, and His name is the Word of God." You can find Jesus and His beautiful nature in the Word and further cultivate your relationship with Him.

- I am a huge advocate of reading the entire Word, not just parts. However, we often read the Bible through distorted lenses. If we think that God is a punishing, unhappy God we will, most likely, find that in the Word. However, the more we move into our God-given identity and our perceptions of Him align more with His nature of being kind and loving, we will see His heart throughout the Scriptures, including the Old Testament. In the meantime, ask Him where to start reading. It may be the Psalms or the Gospels.

- 1 Corinthians 2:9-16 indicates that the things of the Spirit have to be evaluated spiritually. We have to know how to evaluate the Word spiritually. It says, "...the person without the Spirit does not accept the things that come from the Spirit of God but considers them foolishness..." (NIV – verse 14) If you've invited Jesus into your heart, He has made your life His home. You have the best Teacher living inside you! Ask Him to help you begin to understand and evaluate the Word spiritually.

- Surrender your interpretations of the Word to the Holy Spirit. The Bible says that all Scripture is God-breathed. Since He's the One who inspired the Word, He's the best One to interpret the

Word. There are many doctrines that have been birthed from noble pursuits in theology. Sometimes in our attempt to understand the Word, however, we interject our ego into the text and extract something God never intended. A good litmus test for healthy interpretation is whether what we glean from the Word lines up with His loving nature.

- Faith comes by hearing and hearing by the Word of God (Romans 10:17). There is no genuine Christian walk without faith. As we cultivate our Christ-life, the Word of God builds up our new man and deposits faith into our hearts. Faith is counterintuitive to our old man. Hebrews 11:6 says, "Now without faith it is impossible to please God…" As we seek to delight God's heart with our lives, faith is a way of saying, "I love you and I trust you."

- Create your own amplified version. Using concordances and lexicons, seek out the original Hebrew, Aramaic, or Greek words and meanings and create your own translation to help apply what you're reading. I love the verse, "Train up a child in the way he should go: and when he is old, he will not depart from it."[108] One day, I created my own version of this verse to better understand how raising my son in the ways of the Kingdom will keep him anchored in the Lord. This is what I came up with, "Give a child a taste for the things of the Kingdom and in the end nothing will satisfy his palate but the things of God."

Ask Holy Spirit!

The purpose of this manual has been to equip you with building blocks for hearing God's voice and interpreting what He's saying. However, as 1 John 2:27 says, the Holy Spirit is the One who will teach you. He's your ultimate guide. I tell our students that I don't want them to regurgitate what I teach or try to copy what I do. No robots! My heart is that they each work out their own salvation.

I am certainly not advocating rebellion or saying that we don't need covering by godly leaders. What I am saying is that, like the Bereans, we need to search these things out for ourselves to decide whether or not what we're being taught is true (see Acts 17:10-11). Ask the Holy Spirit to guide you. He is the only One who will guide you into all truth. He will teach you how to hear His voice and He will also teach you to discern the real from the counterfeit.

Pursue the Pursuit

Everything God shows you and tells you is an invitation into deeper relationship with the One who created all things. He wants to show you more of His world. Don't let anyone or anything ever put you down or hold you back from being genuinely hungry or curious. Drink deeply! Those who are desperate for the things of God create a place of faith in which He will happily occupy.

Even if you don't have an answer as to "why" you want to know something about God or His world, don't let that stop you or disqualify you! Remember to approach the things of God like a little child, with implicit trust, excitement, and expectation. Stay hungry and stay close to the Holy Spirit. Revelation will surely come.

Just like a parent who waits for the appropriate and right time to open a child's understanding on a matter, God is the same way. He often waits until we are ready before He reveals understanding. This usually happens by the nature of our asking and heart position. Often, our inquiry demonstrates our readiness.

Compare notes with friends, people with whom you know are walking in the same stuff. Sometimes their revelation can bring a greater understanding to yours! That's why we are a Body. We were designed for fellowship and community. We were never meant to be loners.

Keep in mind, that each one of us has a unique expression of the Spirit. It's ok, and perfectly legal, to pursue what someone else carries (especially as a demonstration of a desire for increase or impartation in that area). But don't pursue someone else's grace at the expense of yours. Competition, negligence, jealousy, or comparison, can rob you of the unique expression of the Spirit that God has put within you.

One way to know what to pursue, explore, or search out of the things of God is to ask yourself some questions:

- What things intrigue me in the spiritual matters?
- What things have often confused me?
- What things have been riddled with fear?
- What things, in society for instance, make me really mad?
- What Scriptures have confounded, yet ironically, drawn me?

These are most likely things you are meant to explore. You can know they are covered in God's grace. He's begging you to search them out. The Holy Spirit is highlighting these things, your spirit is discerning it, and God is waiting with answers!

Discernment for Direction

What am I called to? What direction do I go? What is the grace that's available for my life? These are questions we all have. And they are questions that the Lord has answers to. When he was young, our son insightfully said, "Mommy you have to be really quiet to hear God in your heart."

Much of hearing from the Lord is about being still, listening, and discerning. Jeremiah 29:11-13 says, "'For I know the plans I have for you'—this is the Lord's declaration — 'plans for your welfare, not for disaster, to give you a future and a hope. You will call to Me and come and pray to Me, and I will listen to you. You will seek Me and find Me when you search for Me with all your heart. I will be found by you.'" We've all heard this verse a thousand times, right? We often resort to this verse in a time of distress or near hopeless, begging God for breakthrough.

But we can press in to God for His plans for our lives at any time. The key to a Scripture like this is the application. We can daily engage with the Lord regarding His plan for our lives. In fact, in Jeremiah 33:3 He says that if we call to Him, He will answer. That's His promise to us. He *will* answer. Romans 11:29 says, "For the gifts and the calling of God are irrevocable." (NKJV) This means that you have gifts and a call on your life that no person or circumstance can take away.

Some of us have a pretty good understanding of what we're called to in life. Others of us have no clue. Yet, the Bible gives us promises about God showing us which way to go. God has a divine purpose for every person on the planet. Proverbs 3:5-6 says, "Trust in the Lord with all your heart, and do not rely on your own understanding; think about Him in all your ways, and He will guide you on the right paths." When we purpose within ourselves to trust Him and not rely on our own ability to get us to destiny, He'll show us how to get there.

Often, to get us to our purpose, call, or destiny, God will take us on what our logical mind might consider "detours." We must trust His Voice in our lives no matter how illogical it seems. Trusting Him in the process of getting us from A to B requires that we know and hear His voice.

Blind trust is good, but an engaged trust mixed with faith allows us to partner with Him in confidence. It's a new level of maturity. Trust mixed with faith creates intentionality. As the path of process unfolds in front of us we begin to realize God doesn't do random when it comes to our lives.

Sure, God may have something "randomly" pop into our heads about something He's doing but that's about getting our attention. I would suggest that even that "random" act itself was incredibly intentional.

The bigger the assignment on your life, the greater the equipping. I would argue that God has incredibly big things for every person. God doesn't make insignificant people. However, as I mentioned before, often our level of readiness for more is determined by ourselves alone. As we demonstrate a readiness for promotion, we find that God has already equipped us for the next level. You wouldn't give someone a tiny paintbrush to paint the exterior of a house. Likewise, God equips us with the right tools for the job He's leading us to do.

Our pursuit of direction isn't about our "doing," per se, but listening and following. Psalm 40:6 says, "You do not delight in sacrifice and offering; you open my ears to listen." The sacrifice and offering represents self-effort. Listening is engaging with God.

As I'm seeking direction, these are some of the things that I do to find His voice for my life in a matter or identify His flow of grace:

1. Ask directly.

Sometimes we think hearing from Him is this mysterious thing. However, I've found if I just ask direct questions, He often gives me direct answers.

2. Go back to the last time you know you heard His voice.

If you feel that at some point you stopped hearing His voice, go back to the last time you know you heard from Him and camp out there.

3. Look for an ease.

We don't have to kick down doors to get to destiny. Let Him do all the work. That's what He wants to do anyway. He's created a place for us to have a continual rest (see Hebrews 4:9). Often an indication of direction is a place where things easily open up.

4. Thankfulness goes a long way.

Praise Him and thank Him for Who He is. Sometimes we can get so caught up in ourselves that we get our focus off of Him. Praising Him and thanking Him has a way of recalibrating our priorities.

5. Look for breadcrumbs.

As I've mentioned throughout this manual, God is always speaking and equipping us. Look for breadcrumbs that He's dropped along the way (over the last six to 12 months or so). You'll see that He's been preparing you for what's next. This can provide a tremendous amount of clarity and insight.

6. Look around you.

Start observing the activity and environments around you. What people has the Lord brought into your life? What passions have emerged in your heart? What senses of "knowing" have developed within you? What things "resonate" with you? He's always working behind the scenes in ways we don't immediately see. However, a change of perspective can help us discover clues.

7. Ask the right questions.

Sometimes we are asking the wrong questions. We might be incessantly asking "when" as He's working on the "what" or "how." Ask God what questions you should be asking. Again, look for an ease and lightness versus trudging or forcing.

8. Be patient.

Habakkuk 2:3 says, "For the revelation awaits an appointed time; it speaks of the end and will not prove false. Though it lingers, wait for it; it will certainly come and will not delay." God is never late. He just doesn't work on our timeline. Be patient and wait for the next step to be revealed by Him. He's working on your behalf for the greatest success.

9. Let God prophesy to you.

As I've said earlier, sometimes I think we've become a generation who values the prophetic word of man over the written or spoken word of God. This is a misalignment. The Word of God *is* prophetic. One of the best ways for Him to prophesy over us is through reading the Word or speaking directly to our hearts during journaling/devotional times. When He highlights a Scripture to you, for instance, you can know it's the Holy Spirit speaking. This "prophetic word" requires no weighing or judging because it came directly from the heart of God to you, without the filter of flesh. Additionally, when you spend time with God and soak in His Presence, you can ask Him questions like, "What is the key verse for my life in this current season?" or "What is the banner over my life right now?" Wait and listen. His banner over us is love, always. But sometimes He has seasonal, strategic banners over us, as well. These words can also give insight into the direction for our lives.

10. Speak or sing in tongues.

What is born of the Spirit is spirit (John 3:5-8). When we speak or sing in a heavenly language, we edify ourselves and, often, get alignment, clarity, or insight into what God's saying or doing in our lives. Speaking or singing in tongues will have lasting fruit and provide breakthrough. Pictures may emerge as you speak in tongues. Let Him unfold the pictures for you, write them down, and ask Him about them. These can be more breadcrumbs for your life.

11. Discern with your spirit.

Often our flesh fights what our spirit knows. Sensing a season shift is discerning with your spirit. It takes maturity to choose where our spirit is being lead versus what our flesh wants to control or sabotage.

In leading a ministry trip with a friend, we connected with a person who was going to set up host homes for us. As the conversation went on, we discovered there was a list of requirements from this person; things that they were expecting us to do differently than a trip that had gone before us. We sensed we were to arrange our own housing because it "felt" (discernment) that we were indebted to this person (paying off the emotional debt of a previous trip) and we didn't want to move backwards. Our discernment alone was enough to let us know which direction to go, but then my friend texted from a Chinese restaurant. She said her fortune cookie read, "Don't look back, move ahead." Prophetically, we knew God was confirming the direction that our spirits had already discerned.

12. Give yourself grace. Learn from past mistakes.

When we proceed with something He's told us "no" on, we learn to obey His voice the next time. Barreling through a delay or caution is usually due to logic or impatience, born out of flesh. Remember, the flesh will profit us nothing. But we can gain a wealth of maturity through past mistakes. Mistakes are okay! Have grace for yourself.

13. Avoid the temptation to think singularly for your life.

Words from the Lord are multi-dimensional. Avoid the temptation to look at them singularly. God is dynamic and has many plans for your life. Live and move and have your being in Him and He will open up worlds you would have never dreamt of.

14. What are you passionate about?

Have you ever wondered, "Ugh! Why does that bug me so much?" It probably means you're called to change it. If you're called to change it, God has given you the keys, gifts, and grace to do so. A key to destiny lies in the passions of your heart.

Cultivate Your Story with God

When I set out to develop these teachings, I got out books from all the authors and teachers I loved, respected, and those who have been an inspiration to me. I sat down to compile their insights and revelation, but the Lord said, "no." He told me to go through my journals from over the years and develop teachings from my own experience.

God wants to do that with you too. He wants to build a rich story and a robust tool box (giftings, character, etc.) with you so that you are equipped for destiny. God cares for you deeply and is championing you towards fullness. He is always looking for ways to set you up for success.

Additionally, many times we are faced with challenges and issues in life and fear, worry, and anxiety kick in. This is an invitation to look back at the history that you've cultivated with God and confront lies you're believing with truth. When has God ever failed you? Describe and journal all the times He's come through. When have "what-ifs" ever really manifested? Building our history with God gives us courage and faith to face any situation and rest in the confidence of knowing that He will always equip, care for, and protect us.

Know the Voice of Your Shepherd

Jesus is kind. John 10:4 says, "...his sheep follow him because they know his voice." (NIV) What voices are we listening to? An indication of the *source* of those things is the fruit they bear in our lives. God will *never* speak to us through a shaming, condemning, or fear-inducing voice. He is a good Dad who always leads us into places of healing and fullness through His kindness.

Our lives are about identifying, listening, and knowing God's voice. Everything flows from this. Listening to His voice takes a sharp spirit, quiet, intentional soul, and the guidance of the Holy Spirit. Be intentional about discerning the different thoughts throughout your day and taking thoughts captive that don't align with His good nature.[109]

Remember...

There are two very important things to remember on this journey: Pursue Him and pursue love. Colossians 2:3 says, "All the treasures of wisdom and knowledge are hidden in Him." Discovering our spiritual gifts is about discovering God and the beauty of His existence. The more we pursue Him, the more He shows us His world. And we can't discover God without discovering love. You know that you've been transformed by His love when you can extend that to yourself and others. Jesus only gave us one new command: love. He said by this the world will know we belong to Him. Gifts and signs follow love. As we grow in our spiritual gifts, we begin to understand that our pursuit is really a response to an invitation to search Him out, talk with Him, and build relationship with the One who is love.

Reflection

1. What do your times of intimacy with God look like? _____

_____

2. Have there been things that you've been "drawn" to (through the gift of discernment) that you now believe were ways that the Holy Spirit was getting your attention and/or your spirit instinctively knew? If so, what are they?

_____

_____

3. How do you get into the Word? _____

_____

4. What things of the Spirit have intrigued you but you've had a bit of fear or confusion about?

_____

_____

Activation

Activation #1

Seek out testimonies of God supernaturally healing people. What were the illnesses or ailments? What did the healing do to the person's heart? Meet with God and let Him know that you are available to pray for people for supernatural healing.

Activation #2

Write down 3-5 ways that God has been faithful to you over the last two years. Start to be intentional about building your story with Him.

Activation #3

Find a favorite verse in the Bible and do your own amplified version. Use a resource, such as blueletterbible.org, to utilize a concordance and lexicon to help you create one that impacts you.

Activation #4

Spend some time with God and ask Him what specific banner is over your life in this present season. Ask Him what He's equipping you with. Write down what you receive.

Appendix

Testimonies

I love to hear testimonies of what God is doing in your lives! As you've walked through this manual and completed the activations, please let me know what testimonies you have as a result of your learning to grow in spiritual gifts and building your own dictionary. Please email them to klministries@outlook.com or post them to the FB ministry page at Kingdom Leadership Ministries.

Dream Interpretation

What interpretation did you come up with for my dream in the last activation on pages 119 - 120? Email me. I'd love to hear what insight you received.

Contact Information

For more information about booking an equipping school, speaking engagement, or leadership training, please send an inquiry to:

klministries@outlook.com

Or visit Facebook: Kingdom Leadership Ministries

About the Author

Marla Monk believes that all of life flows from a place of love, both for God and people. She is passionate about training and equipping people in the ways of the Kingdom, with a very practical approach, so they can carry gifts and principles into every sphere of influence for Kingdom transformation. Her heart is to awaken individuals, churches, cities, and regions to destiny through preaching, teaching, prophetic ministry, and the supernatural. Marla is the founder of Kingdom Leadership Ministries, a ministry focused on training leaders and extending the Kingdom in the earth through global equipping schools. She currently serves as Director at the School of Kingdom Purpose and oversees the Personal Prophetic Ministry at Church for the Nations in Phoenix, AZ. Prior to Arizona, she and her family lived in Redding, CA where she completed ministry training at BSSM. During her time there, she also interned in the school and was involved in various volunteer leadership roles. Marla has a Bachelor's degree in English and spent over 12 years in the business world, most recently in Human Resources management, before being called to full-time ministry.

Holy Spirit Highlights/Notes

_____

_____

_____

_____

_____

_____

_____

_____

_____

_____

_____

_____

_____

_____

_____

Holy Spirit Highlights/Notes

Holy Spirit Highlights/Notes

Holy Spirit Highlights/Notes

Endnotes

1 Chinese proverb.

2 Dictionary.com. "Eros." Accessed January 28, 2017, http://www.dictionary.com/browse/eros

3 Strong's Exhaustive Concordance: King James Version. 1984. Blue Letter Bible. Accessed January 28, 2017, https://www.blueletterbible.org/lang/lexicon/lexicon.cfm?strongs=G5361&t=KJV

4 Strong's Exhaustive Concordance: King James Version. 1984. Blue Letter Bible. Accessed January 28, 2017, https://www.blueletterbible.org/lang/lexicon/lexicon.cfm?Strongs=G25&t=KJV

5 Psalm 34:8

6 1 John 4:18

7 Revelation 11:15

8 Matthew 6:10

9 Hebrews 1:3

10 Strong's Exhaustive Concordance: King James Version. 1984. Blue Letter Bible. Accessed January 28, 2017, https://www.blueletterbible.org/lang/lexicon/lexicon.cfm?Strongs=G1377&t=KJV

11 John 16:13

12 Anonymous

13 1 John 4:18

14 John 6:63

15 Strong's Exhaustive Concordance: King James Version. 1984. Blue Letter Bible. Accessed January 28, 2017, https://www.blueletterbible.org/lang/lexicon/lexicon.cfm?strongs=G143&t=KJV

16 Strong's Exhaustive Concordance: King James Version. 1984. "Outline of Biblical Usage." Larry Pierce, Online Bible. Blue Letter Bible. Accessed January 28, 2017, https://www.blueletterbible.org/lang/lexicon/lexicon.cfm?Strongs=G1128&t=KJV

17 Watchman Nee.

18 Dr. Allen McCray has been a chief facilitator in my own personal soul healing. The anointing he carries for transformation in this area is remarkable. I highly recommend his books and teachings.

19 Strong's Exhaustive Concordance: King James Version. 1984. Blue Letter Bible. Accessed January 28, 2017, https://www.blueletterbible.org/lang/lexicon/lexicon.cfm?strongs=G5485&t=KJV

20 Mark 16:18

21 Strong's Exhaustive Concordance: King James Version. 1984. "Outline of Biblical Usage." Larry Pierce, Online Bible. Blue Letter Bible. Accessed January 28, 2017. https://www.blueletterbible.org/lang/lexicon/lexicon.cfm?Strongs=G4678&t=KJV

[22] Strong's Exhaustive Concordance: King James Version. 1984. "Outline of Biblical Usage." Larry Pierce, Online Bible. Blue Letter Bible. Accessed January 28, 2017, https://www.blueletterbible.org/lang/lexicon/lexicon.cfm?Strongs=G4102&t=KJV

[23] Strong's Exhaustive Concordance: King James Version. 1984. Blue Letter Bible. Accessed January 28, 2017, https://www.blueletterbible.org/lang/lexicon/lexicon.cfm?strongs=G2390&t=KJV

[24] Strong's Exhaustive Concordance: King James Version. 1984. Blue Letter Bible. Accessed January 28, 2017, https://www.blueletterbible.org/lang/lexicon/lexicon.cfm?Strongs=G1755&t=KJV. Ibid G1411.

[25] Strong's Exhaustive Concordance: King James Version. 1984. "Outline of Biblical Usage." Larry Pierce, Online Bible. Blue Letter Bible. Accessed January 28, 2017, https://www.blueletterbible.org/lang/lexicon/lexicon.cfm?Strongs=G4394&t=KJV. Ibid G4396

[26] Strong's Exhaustive Concordance: King James Version. 1984. Larry Pierce, Online Bible. Blue Letter Bible. Accessed January 28, 2017, https://www.blueletterbible.org/lang/lexicon/lexicon.cfm?Strongs=G1253&t=KJV. Ibid G1252.

[27] Ibid G1252

[28] Strong's Exhaustive Concordance: King James Version. 1984. "Outline of Biblical Usage." Larry Pierce, Online Bible. Blue Letter Bible. Accessed January 28, 2017, https://www.blueletterbible.org/lang/lexicon/lexicon.cfm?Strongs=G1100&t=KJV

[29] Strong's Exhaustive Concordance: King James Version. 1984. Blue Letter Bible. Accessed January 28, 2017, https://www.blueletterbible.org/lang/lexicon/lexicon.cfm?Strongs=G2058&t=KJV

[30] Pastor Bill Johnson has been a catalyst and great inspiration for me, especially in the teaching and treasuring of this passage in Isaiah, in apprehending the heart and spirit of what God is doing in the earth to transform nations.

[31] Ibid G1243

[32] Strong's Exhaustive Concordance: King James Version. 1984. "Outline of Biblical Usage." Larry Pierce, Online Bible. Blue Letter Bible. Accessed January 28, 2017, https://www.blueletterbible.org/lang/lexicon/lexicon.cfm?Strongs=G1838&t=KJV

[33] Strong's Exhaustive Concordance: King James Version. 1984. "Outline of Biblical Usage." Larry Pierce, Online Bible. Blue Letter Bible. Accessed January 28, 2017, https://www.blueletterbible.org/lang/lexicon/lexicon.cfm?Strongs=G145&t=KJV. Ibid G143

[34] Strong's Exhaustive Concordance: King James Version. 1984. "Outline of Biblical Usage." Larry Pierce, Online Bible. Blue Letter Bible. Accessed January 28, 2017, https://www.blueletterbible.org/lang/lexicon/lexicon.cfm?Strongs=H8085&t=KJV. Ibid G191

[35] Ibid G1492

[36] Ibid H2596

[37] Ibid G3744

[38] Strong's Exhaustive Concordance: King James Version. 1984. "Outline of Biblical Usage." Larry Pierce, Online Bible. Blue Letter Bible. Accessed January 28, 2017. https://www.blueletterbible.org/lang/lexicon/lexicon.cfm?Strongs=G1097&t=KJV

[39] John 3:8

[40] 1 Corinthians 14:33

[41] Ibid H4397

[42] Matthew 9:15 – 17

[43] The material in this section comes from personal experience, revelation and extensive personal study. However, I have been greatly influenced by the teachings of Kris Vallotton and Nancy Cobb at Bethel Church during my four years in Redding, CA, through the process of osmosis, as some of the larger section titles may reflect.

[44] Strong's Exhaustive Concordance: King James Version. 1984. "Outline of Biblical Usage." Larry Pierce, Online Bible. Blue Letter Bible. Accessed January 29, 2017. https://www.blueletterbible.org/lang/lexicon/lexicon.cfm?Strongs=G652&t=KJV

[45] The spheres of influence referenced here come from the teachings of Lance Wallnau (who was influenced by Loren Cunningham, founder of YWAM), Bill Johnson, and Paul Manwaring (during my time at Bethel).

[46] Dr. Michael Maiden, head pastor at Church for the Nations, is a world-class leader in consistently demonstrating love and grace as a priority in the church. My life has been transformed by the standard he sets.

[47] Matthew 10:8

[48] Strong's Exhaustive Concordance: King James Version. 1984. "Outline of Biblical Usage." Larry Pierce, Online Bible. Blue Letter Bible. Accessed January 29, 2017. https://www.blueletterbible.org/lang/lexicon/lexicon.cfm?strongs=G1430&t=KJV

[49] Ibid G3874

[50] Ibid G3889

[51] Numbers 22:21-39

[52] Strong's Exhaustive Concordance: King James Version. 1984. "Outline of Biblical Usage." Larry Pierce, Online Bible. Blue Letter Bible. Accessed February 25, 2017. https://www.blueletterbible.org/lang/lexicon/lexicon.cfm?Strongs=H7200&t=KJV

[53] Ibid H7200

[54] 1 Corinthians 2:16

[55] Strong's Exhaustive Concordance: King James Version. 1984. "Outline of Biblical Usage." Larry Pierce, Online Bible. Blue Letter Bible. Accessed January 29, 2017. https://www.blueletterbible.org/lang/lexicon/lexicon.cfm?Strongs=H8085&t=KJV

[56] Ibid H559

[57] 1 Corinthians 9:22

[58] 1 Peter 4:11

[59] 1 Peter 4:8

[60] Ibid G4487

[61] Strong's Exhaustive Concordance: King James Version. 1984. "Outline of Biblical Usage." Larry Pierce, Online Bible. Blue Letter Bible. Accessed January 29, 2017. https://www.blueletterbible.org/lang/lexicon/lexicon.cfm?Strongs=G3857&t=KJV

[62] Ibid H4236

[63] Ibid H4759

[64] Ibid H2377

[65] Ibid G1611

[66] Ibid G3701

[67] Ibid G602

[68] John 13:23

[69] Strong's Exhaustive Concordance: King James Version. 1984. Blue Letter Bible. Accessed January 29, 2017. https://www.blueletterbible.org/lang/lexicon/lexicon.cfm?Strongs=H2830&t=KJV

[70] Dictionary.com. "Synesthesia." Accessed January 29, 2017. http://www.dictionary.com/browse/synesthesia?s=t

[71] Kirkpatrick, George. *The Types and Symbols of the Bible.* 1988. Accessed January 29, 2017 (originally searched March 15, 2009). http://www.newfoundationspubl.org/types.htm (adaptation)

[72] Ibid

[73] 2 Corinthians 3:18

[74] James 5:16

[75] Strong's Exhaustive Concordance: King James Version. 1984. "Outline of Biblical Usage." Larry Pierce, Online Bible. Blue Letter Bible. Accessed January 29, 2017. https://www.blueletterbible.org/lang/lexicon/lexicon.cfm?Strongs=H2472&t=KJV

[76] Luke 6:45

[77] James 2:13

[78] Psalm 97:2

[79] The material in this chapter comes from personal experience, revelation, and study. Some information in this section has been adapted from personal notes taken from dream teachings of Crystal Stiles (via John Paul Jackson).

[80] Some of the dream topics in this section have been influenced by dream teachings of Crystal Stiles (via John Paul Jackson) and James W. and Michal Ann Goll from their book, *Dream Language.* Pages 103 – 111. Destiny Image Publishers, Inc. 2006.

[81] 1 Peter 5:6

[82] Gaither, William J. "There's Something About That Name." 1970.

[83] Dictionary.com. "Metaphor." Accessed December 22, 2016. http://www.dictionary.com/browse/metaphor?s=t

[84] Dictionary.com. "Symbolism." Accessed December 22, 2016. http://www.dictionary.com/browse/symbolism?s=t

[85] Genesis 37:9-11

[86] Genesis 37:5-8; Genesis 42:5-6

[87] Some information in this section has been adapted from personal notes taken from dream teachings of Crystal Stiles (via John Paul Jackson).

[88] John 14:16; Greek word for Counselor is *paraklētos*. G3875

[89] Strong's Exhaustive Concordance: King James Version. 1984. Blue Letter Bible. Accessed January 29, 2017. https://www.blueletterbible.org/lang/lexicon/lexicon.cfm?Strongs=G4856&t=KJV

[90] Ibid G1162

[91] Ibid G4336

[92] G2169

[93] Ibid 2172

[94] The material in this chapter is from personal experience, revelation, and study. However, Dutch Sheets has been a hero of mine regarding the topic of intercession. I immersed myself in his audio teachings, "Intercessory Prayer – The Lightning of God!" 1993. Additionally, I've been greatly influenced by his book, *Intercessory Prayer*. Regal Books. 1996. I highly recommend both for further study on the topic.

[95] Strong's Exhaustive Concordance: King James Version. 1984. Blue Letter Bible. Accessed January 29, 2017. https://www.blueletterbible.org/lang/lexicon/lexicon.cfm?Strongs=G2540&t=KJV

[96] Ibid G5550

[97] Ibid H6293

[98] Strong's Exhaustive Concordance: King James Version. 1984. "Outline of Biblical Usage." Larry Pierce, Online Bible. Blue Letter Bible. Accessed January 29, 2017. https://www.blueletterbible.org/lang/lexicon/lexicon.cfm?Strongs=H6293&t=KJV

[99] Strong's Exhaustive Concordance: King James Version. 1984. "Outline of Biblical Usage." Larry Pierce, Online Bible. Blue Letter Bible. Accessed January 29, 2017. https://www.blueletterbible.org/lang/lexicon/lexicon.cfm?Strongs=G1783&t=KJV

[100] Peter Furler. "Everyone's Someone." *Love Liberty Disco*. Newsboys. Sparrow Records, 1999. CD.

[101] Strong's Exhaustive Concordance: King James Version. 1984. "Outline of Biblical Usage." Larry Pierce, Online Bible. Blue Letter Bible. Accessed January 29, 2017. https://www.blueletterbible.org/lang/lexicon/lexicon.cfm?Strongs=G2807&t=KJV

[102] Romans 4:17

[103] Luke 10:18

[104] Psalm 84:5

[105] A. A. Milne. *Winnie-the-Pooh*. Methuen & Co. Ltd. London. 1926

[106] James 1:17

[107] Judy Franklin and Ellyn Davis. *Physics of Heaven*. Page 76. Double Portion Publishing. 2012.

[108] Proverbs 22:6

[109] 2 Corinthians 10:1-6